THE BIBLE FOR SINNERS

Interpretation in the present time

Christopher Rowland and
Jonathan Roberts

SPCK

First published in Great Britain in 2008

Society for Promoting Christian Knowledge
36 Causton Street
London SW1P 4ST

British Library Cataloguing-in-Publication Data
A catalogue record for this book is available from the British Library

ISBN 978–0–281–05802–0

1 3 5 7 9 10 8 6 4 2

Typeset by Graphicraft Ltd, Hong Kong
Printed in Great Britain by Ashford Colour Press

Produced on paper from sustainable forests

To Emma Mason

Contents

Acknowledgements		vi
A note on terms		vii
1	The Bible for gluttons, drunkards and other 'sinners'	1
2	'Christian' responses to same-sex relationships	13
3	Interpretation in context	30
4	Liberation Theology	45
5	Christian radicals: Denck and Winstanley	61
6	Christian radicals: Blake and Stringfellow	73
7	Marriage and divorce	88
8	Concluding reflections	103
Glossary		107
Notes		109
Suggestions for further reading		114
Index		116

Acknowledgements

———◆———

Ruth McCurry first suggested this book to us, and we have been grateful of her patience and critical solidarity throughout the writing of it. Zoë Bennett and her students in the Cambridge Theological Federation provided material for an earlier version of one of the chapters and we are grateful for her co-operation and understanding when we decided to use the material differently. John Lewis and Jane Patterson from the Center for Faith in the Workplace offered helpful feedback and reflections on the manuscript, as did Ying Roberts, Catherine Rowland, Roy Dorey, Neville Black and Eric Szmyt. Carol Roberts kindly suggested some of the dialogue in Chapter 7. We wish to express our thanks to all of these people. The list of writers who have inspired particular sections of this book is much longer, and a few of those names can be found in the 'Suggestions for further reading' at the end of this work.

The authors' royalties are being paid to Oxfam.

A note on terms

We have tried to avoid too much unfamiliar terminology in this book though we do rely on three terms – exegesis, hermeneutics and Sachkritik – in our discussion. These terms will be familiar to many readers, but for those to whom they are new we have put a short glossary (along with a few other key terms) at the back of the book.

We use the terms 'context' and 'contextual theology' throughout this book. For many writers 'context' refers to the words which immediately precede or follow a particular biblical passage. So, within a discussion of the Bible, 'context' could refer to the wider setting of a passage; to the book in which it is found; to either the Old or New Testament; or to the Bible as a whole. The term 'context' is also widely used to indicate the social and political context within which reading takes place, and it is this meaning that we usually refer to by 'context' and 'contextual theology' in this book.

Now all the tax-collectors and sinners were coming near to listen to him. And the Pharisees and the scribes were grumbling and saying, 'This fellow welcomes sinners and eats with them'.

Luke 15.1–2

For John the Baptist has come eating no bread and drinking no wine, and you say, 'He has a demon'; the Son of Man has come eating and drinking, and you say, 'Look, a glutton and a drunkard, a friend of tax-collectors and sinners!'

Luke 7.33–34 and Matthew 11.18–19

You hypocrites! You know how to interpret the appearance of earth and sky, but why do you not know how to interpret the present time?

Luke 12.56

1

The Bible for gluttons, drunkards and other 'sinners'

In perhaps his most famous parable, Jesus asks his listeners to imagine a man beaten up, robbed and left by the roadside, while a Levite and priest pass him by and do nothing to help. What kind of mindset is that?

Imagine that you are a priest. You have committed yourself to God's service. You meditate upon the ancestral traditions night and day. You give money to the poor and to God's work. Part of your calling is to interpret these traditions and you do this prayerfully. You are attempting to preserve and to hand on to others the sacred tradition that you have inherited. Imagine now that someone appears on the scene, a radical, transgressing and subverting the tradition, and making a point of doing so publicly and confrontationally. He is not part of the tradition, he has no right to speak the way he does, he is influencing and misleading many people. He fraternizes with gluttons, drunkards and other sinners. This situation that has arisen poses a real threat to your faith, to the sanctity of your religion: is it not, therefore, your obligation, your religious duty to stand up and speak out against this transgressor?

This is, of course, the position of Jesus' opponents in the Gospels, but it is also the difficult position occupied by many people within the Church today. Like Jesus' opponents, they wish to preserve tradition and obey the commandments, yet they also recognize that in his own day Jesus was himself rejected by people who held just such an outlook. It is fitting, in the light of this, that Jesus is reported to have said that he came to bring not peace but a sword, and that he would divide people, even within families. This double-edged aspect of his own ministry is reflected in divisions among those who seek to follow him. It is most evident when new, difficult, and above all else *human* situations and dilemmas arise.

At such times, many people feel compelled to look to the past and to follow 'tradition', yet faced with the same scenarios others will look to the situation as one in which the Spirit of God may be saying something new. Examples of these contrasting positions are not hard to find. This book is written in a situation in which the Anglican Church, a communion of over 70 million adherents in 161 countries, is acrimoniously divided over issues of human sexuality and their relation to the humanity of individuals: does the sexual orientation of an individual preclude them from serving as a minister of God? And – more recently – does it preclude such individuals from consideration as adopting parents?

The Church is an ancient and hierarchical institution, and it tends towards the side of 'tradition' in the face of new challenges. This is by no means universally the case – the ordination of women priests is a powerful counter-example – but it does tend to mean that the voice of tradition is powerfully articulated in new debates and often seems to have all the resources on its side. After all, traditional Anglican theology grounds itself in scripture, tradition and reason. Tradition, as a consequence, is often the loudest voice, but it has never been the only one. This book is not an attempt to devalue tradition or the insights of those in the ecclesiastical hierarchy, but it does attempt to listen to other voices and to consider what alternative resources might be appealed to when such debates arise.

In presenting this material we are considering alternatives to the sorts of answers usually handed down from 'above' (by those, for example, in ecclesiastical power). This is not contrariness on our part but is, we believe, central to Christianity itself, because while there are clearly precedents for appealing to tradition in the Bible, there are also precedents (including the reported examples of Jesus himself) for refuting traditions in the face of new situations, and choosing instead to look for the guidance of the Spirit. Jesus pushes his listeners to think again about the relationship between their inherited understandings and their current life situations: rounding on his opponents he demands – in the words we have used in our title – 'you know how to interpret the appearance of earth and sky, but why do you not know how to interpret the present time?' (Luke 12.56).

The role of the Bible

The two positions sketched above (which might be characterized as 'trust in tradition' and 'trust in the Spirit') are both rooted in the Bible, which will always be a key element in such debates. Faced with new challenges, Christians will want to look to the Bible (just as Jesus' opponents looked to their own scriptures), yet this is never simply a case of 'applying' the Bible. As all traditions recognize, the Bible needs to be interpreted, and by that very fact we are in continuing dialogue and negotiation with scripture – it cannot simply dictate to us what we should do in our complex and ever-changing life situations.

Quite the reverse: negotiating in what way the Bible can help, and being realistic about the limitations of that process are crucial to our journey. There is no quick fix here: as William Blake saw so clearly, the Bible is as much part of the problem as the solution, and even the most conservative fundamentalist will have to struggle to work out some kind of rationale for its interpretation. The question then comes down to 'Who has the right to interpret?' Can I seek to gain understanding from within a situation (guided by the Spirit), or should I look for answers that come from outside that situation – from, say, ecclesiastical tradition?

An example from the Catholic tradition

The significance of this question can be illustrated in relation to the issue of contraception and HIV/AIDS. The Catholic Church has an ancient theological tradition (rooted in Genesis and Aquinas) which forbids the use of contraception on the basis that human sexuality should ideally be oriented towards procreation, and never 'artificially' interfered with. In Pope John Paul's words:

> [W]hen there is a reason not to procreate, this choice is permissible and may even be necessary. However, there remains the duty of carrying it out with criteria and methods that respect the total truth of the marital act in its unitive and procreative dimension, as wisely regulated by nature itself in its biological rhythms. One can comply with them and use them to advantage, but they cannot be 'violated' by artificial interference.[1]

No one doubts either the theological sincerity of tradition or its internal logic. The Catholic position on contraception has existed for many centuries, but the complication is that in the interim the world has changed. AIDS, a very recent disease, currently kills an estimated 2.8 million people a year,[2] and in the light of this reality it is much more difficult to specify the forbidding of contraception – a key element in the fight against the spread of HIV – as something 'Christian'.

Here then is a hard example of a tradition speaking from above or beyond a situation both in time and place. What is the alternative? In this case, should an interpretation of the right path for Christians be made from within the situation? Could it be right, for example, for those with AIDS or working with those with AIDS to revisit the question of contraception in the light of their experience and to think again about how the Bible speaks to this situation? Faced with the human realities of the AIDS pandemic, many Christians would say that interpretation from 'within' the situation might in this case be right. However, this is a difficult move when the tradition in question understands itself to be the primary medium through which

God speaks to the modern world. If it comes to a disagreement, the question is raised: what right do sinners and nobodies, individuals with their own agendas – people, in fact, in similar positions to that of Jesus – have to interpret the Bible in the light of their own experience? Shouldn't we get our interpretations from those above and before us, our moral or religious betters?

'Sinners' and the right to interpret

The key difference between the two types of interpretation outlined above lies in the question of authority. More particularly, the concept of authority (in both Anglican and Catholic cases) is related to the concept of traditions sanctified, as it were, by righteousness. This is in accordance with both ecclesiastical and public conceptions of what Christianity has come to mean. The difficulty for such a view is, of course, that Jesus himself is deemed unfit to teach (in the eyes of his opponents) by his association with gluttons, drunkards and other sinners. He himself eats and drinks with sinners, is called 'a glutton and a drunkard', and in the eyes of his opponents his inability to tell who is righteous and who is a sinner – and to keep an appropriate distance from the latter – demonstrates his unfitness to interpret scripture:

> John the Baptist came neither eating bread nor drinking wine, and you say, 'He has a demon.' The Son of Man came eating and drinking, and you say, 'Here is a glutton and a drunkard, a friend of tax collectors and "sinners".' (Luke 7.33–34)

Our book addresses this question of how moral judgements are sometimes used – of ourselves and others – as a basis for the right to interpret scripture. This, then, is the point of our book's title: does the accusation of sinfulness prevent us from meaningfully engaging in biblical interpretation? It would, we suggest, severely limit the Bible's ability to speak to us if we seek its help because of our 'sinfulness' but by that very fact are precluded from interpreting it by relating it to our own situations.

The interplay of these different elements – tradition, the Spirit, the Bible, moral judgement – can be difficult to discern, and our aim is to proceed by example rather than abstraction. We therefore begin the book with a key public voice speaking on the relationship between the Bible and life: Bishop Tom Wright. Wright is centrally interested in the questions of tradition and authority and their relationship to interpretation, as the title of his recent book *Scripture and the Authority of God* suggests. We look to Wright's example not only because of his clear views on 'authority' in scripture and tradition, but also because he is perhaps the best-known spokesperson of evangelical Anglicanism within the UK today. He is a best-selling author (of over 30 books), and an active public speaker. Through these and other channels he has significant influence on the Church worldwide, on individuals who read his work, and on public perception of the social issues on which he speaks.

Tom Wright's model of interpretation

In a lecture entitled 'How Can the Bible be Authoritative?'[3] Wright offers a useful analogy to how Christians might live with the Bible. He asks us to imagine that a Shakespeare play exists whose fifth (and final) act has been lost. A group of sensitive and experienced Shakespearean actors immerse themselves in the first four acts and then have to work out a fifth act for themselves in the light of all that they know about the play and about Shakespeare's work. In this scenario, Wright says, the first four acts have clear authority for the task in hand, but it is an 'authority' that requires consistency and innovation rather than unthinking repetition of the earlier parts of the play. For the drama to work, there must be development and something new in the fifth act. In his biblical analogy, Wright suggests that the first four acts correlate to Creation, Fall, Israel and Jesus, with the New Testament forming the first scene in the fifth act. The analogy is useful, he suggests, because the Church lives under the authority of the existing story which cannot be supplanted or supplemented, and yet, 'Our task is to discover, through the Spirit and prayer, the appropriate ways of improvising the script between the foundation events and charter on the one hand and the complete coming of the kingdom on the other.'[4]

This helpful analogy reminds us of the situation we are in when trying to relate the Bible to present-day life situations, given that our understandings are always partial and provisional. We have a sense of religious history that we may try to relate to: theologically speaking, we know what has happened, and may hope – at least in general terms – for what the ending might be, but we don't know how we get to that ending, and in the meantime what is needed, as Wright suggests, is 'improvisation'. The idea of improvisation is a daring one because it is open to life, to the incorporation of new experiences and new understandings. As Wright recognizes, drama is all about a journey into the unknown, and moments of utter surprise – such as the resurrection of Jesus – are the essence of the Christian story. After all, in the picture of the last judgement in Matthew 25 both righteous and unrighteous are surprised about the outcome.

Improvisation means that we need to negotiate a way forward that is attentive to the biblical themes that have already been set forth, but we are in no way bound to follow them to the letter. The lot of those of us who are negotiating unmapped terrain is to create a way forward utilizing our knowledge of the past and our collective experience, but without assuming that the answers appropriate to the past are going to be those of the present. Crucial to our understanding of the situation we are in is the promise of Jesus that the Spirit will guide into all truth (John 16.13), even if that means 'more than you can now bear' (John 16.12). So, discerning what that truth is, is not simply a matter of appealing to the past, but discerning what the Spirit is *now* saying to the churches (e.g. Revelation 2.7). The logic of this position is that it cannot be ruled out of court – to take one example – that gay and lesbian relationships may not be part of the divine purpose in the fifth act, whatever may have been the case in other acts of the play.

Wright endorses this openness to new understanding, acknowledging that this space demands of us innovation as well as respect for the past. However, his Shakespearean analogy reveals another, much less open aspect to his hermeneutic (interpretive method). For Wright suggests that in the reconstruction of 'Act Five' of the lost play it is the *experts* that will use their historical and dramatic expertise to reconstruct the plot and its outworking. In ecclesiastical terms, the logic of his analogy is that the 'experts' who make the reconstruction should be the clergy. It is at this point that we part company with him because in the context of the Christian Church (as reflected in 1 Corinthians 12) expertise is not only the prerogative of the theologians, bishops and ecclesial officials.[5]

Collaborative hermeneutics

The God who has poured the Spirit on all flesh (Acts 2.17) empowers all to contribute to the writing of this final act. Indeed, it is one of the contributions of liberation, black and feminist approaches to theology that they have stressed the importance of the perspective of 'outsiders', and the vulnerable and oppressed to the understanding of the divine purpose. Jesus gave thanks that it was the little ones who understood while the wise and learned couldn't get the point (Matthew 11.25). Thus the exclusion of anyone from the fifth act by a prior decision about what the contents of the drama might be (or who should write it), completely undercuts the process of discernment of which we are a part.

In considering these matters this book has two basic themes:

- Negotiating our way through the terrain or reconstructing the 'fifth act' is a collaborative enterprise.
- Love is the ground of that collaboration, and we cannot therefore expect to love God unless we first love our brother or sister.

That is to say, life lived together on earth in mutual support, in justice for the stranger and the outcast as well as support for the vulnerable is the environment for the revelation of God. It is the practice of that love that might enable some kind of insight into the divine will and enable us to chart a better way forward in our earthly pilgrimage, to find the meaning of that fifth act. Albert Schweitzer put it brilliantly in the final paragraphs of *The Quest of the Historical Jesus*:

> He comes to us as One unknown, without a name, as of old, by the lakeside. He came to those men who knew him not. He speaks to us the same words: 'Follow thou me!' and sets us to the tasks which He has to fulfil for our time. He commands. And to those who obey Him, whether they be wise or simple, he will reveal Himself in the toils, the conflicts, the sufferings, which they shall pass through in His fellowship, and as an ineffable mystery, they shall learn in their own experience Who He is.[6]

The function of this book

So, what we seek to do in this book is not to write our own version of the 'fifth act' but to consider how that writing might be done in ways that are attentive to the specifics of particular situations, and that abide (as we do in life) with understandings and solutions that are provisional and human-centred. In one sense, this book does not enter either the liberal or the conservative camp insofar as it is not providing a reading of the Bible. This is the case despite the fact that it deals with some of the most contentious and divisive issues within the Church of recent years, including adultery, same-sex relationships and divorce. In discussing these topics we proceed with an eye to means rather than ends, and reflect on different types of interpretive strategy rather than attempting to assess the truth value of particular acts of biblical interpretation. This book does not, therefore, provide prepared answers that can be taken away on any of its key topics. Instead, each chapter provides a different heuristic (illustrative) discussion as a means to thinking about interpretation, and attempts to illuminate the key differences between open-endedness and closure in acts of interpretation.

Chapter 2 considers the ongoing Anglican debate over clergy in same-sex relationships. It is the first major topic we discuss because of the importance of the hermeneutical issues that this debate has raised and the effect it has had in galvanizing many of us to think afresh about the interpretation of the Bible. The Anglican debate thereby forms a catalyst for much of what follows in this book. The approach we take is to suggest that Christian interpretation of the Bible has always involved trying to discern the way of Christ rather than merely pursuing obedience to this or that principle or precept. That discernment involves an open-minded, imaginative interrelating of biblical text and contemporary situation – a model that is approached in different ways, practical and historical, throughout the rest of the book.

In Chapter 3 we look at ancient and modern ways of reading the Bible alongside a discussion of the nature and limits of literal exegesis. We ask whether modern-day biblical scholarship is as objective, as 'scientific', or indeed as oriented to the literal sense of the text as it claims to be, and we point out the fundamental role of imagination in historical reconstruction. We discuss critical understanding as a common goal of all theological approaches (ancient and modern), and we suggest that critical understanding is particularly evident in the openness to dialogue that comes when those doing the theology attend to their own contexts.

Chapter 4 considers more closely the dialectic between contemporary situation and biblical text by looking at the example of Liberation Theology. As a paradigm of contextual theology, the emphasis on context and experience is central to Liberation Theology, but there is something more too: at the heart of this theology is the belief that it is through commitment and action on behalf of the vulnerable and oppressed that one might begin to understand not only the Bible but also the ways of

God. That means that in its hermeneutical method priority is not given to detachment and separation but to involvement and solidarity.

Chapters 5 and 6 explore the ways in which interpreters on the fringes of mainstream Christianity have taken up the themes of context and experience described in the earlier chapters. Too often, those who have claimed inspiration from the Spirit to do and think something new have ended up being demonized by those who found their views too subversive. Many of them deserve a fairer hearing and more attention as part of the Christian tradition than is the case in most mainstream churches. These two chapters consider four individuals from very different worlds – Hans Denck, Gerrard Winstanley, William Blake and William Stringfellow – who remind us that belief in the Holy Spirit is not another way of asserting orthodoxy but is an openness to the God who makes all things new and who beckons us to share in hope for the future.

Chapter 7 looks at the difficult issues of marriage and divorce, and considers how the Bible, which has been a source of freedom for so many, has become the ground of misery and persecution for others. The discussion articulates different positions on this topic without attempting to resolve them. It is not intended to show one party 'beating' the other, but to suggest alternative strategies of biblical interpretation which offer possibilities for self-reflection, and mutual understanding. 'Failure' or 'success' in this context are irrelevant categorizations.

In summary

What we believe we are setting out in this book is an approach to dealing with texts that is similar to that carried out by the Jesus of the Gospels. We say 'the Jesus of the Gospels' because whatever the totality of their relationship may be with the historical Jesus, there is something about the Gospels which separates them off from other parts of the New Testament, not to mention from the fabric of Christian theology, at least in the

Christian mainstream as it has emerged down the centuries. The Gospels depict a person who was less interested in and pre-occupied with the Bible and tradition than many of his contemporaries. Indeed, his whole approach was characterized by an ambivalent relationship to traditional teaching, and this offers a basic hermeneutical model which we want to try to emulate.

It would be wrong to mistake Jesus' radical interpretations of the Law as a complete rejection of the Law, and we find him from time to time going out of his way to uphold it (Mark 1.44). Nonetheless, he seems to have taken a more lax attitude towards certain practices than many of his contemporaries. One of the issues to which the traditions point as an item of conflict between Jesus and his contemporaries was sabbath observance. In the account of the disciples plucking grain on the sabbath (Mark 2.23ff.) Jesus justifies their actions by reference to scripture, to the act of David (2.25ff.), indicating that when humans are in need, there is justification for breaking the strict sabbath code. As Mark 2.27 makes plain, it is humans who are important, not the keeping of a regulation at any price. Jesus' attitude suggests that rules from the past are there for the promotion of human betterment and if they do not fulfil that task then their role of authority should be questioned. That means, for example, that the sabbath was made for humans and not vice versa.

Jesus was accused of being a drunkard and a glutton and a friend of tax collectors and sinners (Matthew 11.19; Mark 2.16; Luke 7.34), and we are his disciples if we learn to read the witness about him in that spirit. There is something instinctive, immediate and existential about his personal ministry even if the religion he sets in train seems to be so much at odds with that to which he calls us. It is the Gospels' witness to Jesus which, as it were, stands over against us all, challenging the restrictions of ecclesiastical tradition and challenging the conviction that the Church has necessarily got it right more often than it has got it wrong.

2

'Christian' responses to same-sex relationships

———◦———

Can an openly gay man who admits to being in a same-sex relationship become a leader in the Church? This was the issue over the nomination of Jeffrey John in the UK and remains the issue over the appointment of Gene Robinson as Bishop of New Hampshire in the USA. It's a debate that is threatening to split the Anglican Church apart. This is the first major issue we address in this book because, from a hermeneutical perspective, this split exposes a fault-line in modern ways of understanding the Bible. What the debate clarifies is the difference between those who appeal to the Bible as the final word on a given topic, and those who seek to locate current debates within a broader understanding of Christianity of which the biblical text constitutes only one component part. This difference of approach is particularly evident in the debate over homosexuality because unlike the debate about, say, the ordination of women or the equality of people of different ethnic backgrounds in the Church, there is nothing in the Bible that explicitly supports the propriety of gay and lesbian sexual relationships.

In this situation it has been easy for many Christians to fall back on a particular type of hermeneutical strategy which involves resorting to using the biblical text as if it were a court of appeal. This strategy has been widely used by Christians, especially since the Reformation when the Bible became central to the doctrine and teaching of Protestant churches. If this was what Christianity amounted to, if entering a meaningful relationship with God was a matter of simply appealing to 'what the Bible says', then the answer on homosexuality would be clear: no biblical passage condones male homosexuality, and the Bible has nothing explicit to say about lesbian relationships. Things are not, however, that simple. That legalistic appeal to the Bible represents a particular hermeneutical manoeuvre with its own history, and in this book we wish to draw attention to hermeneutical alternatives by suggesting that in trying to get at what it means to be a Christian (according to both the Bible and other Christian texts), resorting to 'what a sacred text says' is never the last word on any subject.

Christians believe in the activity of the divine Spirit in the hearts and lives of humans and the attempt to hear what the Spirit is now saying to the churches requires an openness to human experience in all its diversity (past and present) so that together Christians may grasp the inclusive understanding of human relating that God offers. The open-mindedness and imaginative engagement that Tom Wright rightly asks of us in 'Act Five' means it is essential that we do not foreclose this opportunity by resorting to a conservative legalism.

So, while Christians of a more conservative stance have talked about 'drawing a line in the sand' to demarcate a point where permissiveness stops and the Church has to say 'no further', there are many other Christians who would wish to support the nominations of individuals such as John and Robinson. The latter group are fully aware of passages (such as 1 Corinthians 6 and Romans 1) that the former group point to as irrefutable proof, yet they would nonetheless support such appointments for two reasons. First, they wish to be attentive to what God is calling people to in the fullness of their person-hood. Second, this support echoes what the New Testament offers regarding God's call to all people – of any gender, of any age, of any ethnic background or sexual orientation – to learn to live together in mutual acceptance in community.

The debate has foregrounded not simply particular aspects of the texts and traditions that we have inherited, but also the question of how Christians should relate to them. In seeking a better understanding of those relationships, in this chapter we ask what we might learn from the way early Christians related to the texts and traditions that they inherited. We provide this look at the early Church in order to bring into question the ways in which modern Christians too easily identify the will of God with what is written in the Bible (or for that matter 'what the Church has always taught'). As such, this chapter is less a worked example of a method than an enquiry into the dynamics of early Christian hermeneutics, and is written in order to reflect on how we may seek to discern the lineaments of a hermeneutic from the Bible, and thereby use the Bible as an inspiration rather than as an infallible guide. After considering these examples, we return to the homosexuality debate later in the chapter.

As elsewhere in the book, there is a degree of circularity to our discussion. We are arguing that Christianity is not merely a religion of the book, and yet we are drawing on the Bible as one of our sources in support of this discussion. We are not suggesting that the Bible demands the position we are offering; rather, we are suggesting that it offers many different perspectives, including radical voices, which prevent a simple appeal to the Bible as a univocal authoritative text. The Bible, we are suggesting, provides a model for engaging with difference.

Early Christian writers' use of the Bible

If we want to discern the character of Christ then one component of that process is going to be the Bible. Nevertheless, from the very start of Christian history mere appeal to 'what the Bible says' was never deemed to be an adequate ground for the Christian life. As Christianity sought to offer a message for those outside the bounds of Judaism, it rapidly became necessary to show how Christ might have been involved in the life and thought of all people. Early Christian writers did this through the *logos* doctrine; that is, by stressing that the divine Word was already active in the lives of men and women centuries before, without their ever being part of the people of God.

15

The opening of the Gospel of John, which speaks of the true light enlightening everyone coming into the world, broadened the horizons of the activity of Christ beyond the records of Jesus' life given in the pages of the Gospel.

When seeking to discern what may be of God and what not, early Christian writers used a complex mix of appeal to tradition, to recognized forebears of the way, and to what they termed 'a rule of faith': a simple formula, probably the forerunner of the Christian creeds, which offered a benchmark for those who would select true teaching from false. This mix was never simply an appeal to the past, something which from the very start had never been at the heart of Christianity. After all, the origins of Christianity lay in a radically new reading of received wisdom, claiming a degree of continuity with earlier scriptures but never allowing what had been written in the past to determine what God's Spirit was calling people to in the present. It is here that the Christian conviction – that the Spirit, among other things, opens up the meaning of the letters of scripture – comes into play (cf. 2 Corinthians 3.6).

We now give three brief examples from within the Bible and early Christianity in which the sort of hermeneutical strategy that we are advocating is deployed; which is to say, three situations in which attention to the Spirit and compassion towards one's fellow humans was prioritized over a legalistic adherence to scripture.

1 Jesus and authority

Within the Judaism of Jesus' day there were many different interpretations of what constituted obedience to God. According to Mark 1.22 (cf. 11.28), Jesus' teaching differed from that of the scribes, and the distinctive feature about it was its authority. At the heart of the scribal and rabbinic religion was the belief that their discernment of the divine will in their context was no novelty but could be traced back in its essentials to the prophets and ultimately to Moses himself. (This position is found in the early Jewish collection of sayings from rabbinic teachers known as Pirke Aboth 1:1, which was, roughly speaking, contemporary with the New Testament.) The concern for tradition and the application of insights from the past to the needs of the present is absent from Jesus' teaching, which is marked by an authority which must have seemed arrogant to some of his contemporaries.

The interpretations of the Law of Moses in the Sermon on the Mount (Matthew 5.21ff.; cf. Mark 2.6), for example, make no reference to previous doctrinal authorities, but introduce the interpretations with the emphatic 'I', indicating that Jesus considered himself to be an interpreter at least on a par with the doctrinal authorities of his own day.

The issue of authority also lies behind the Beelzebub controversy (Mark 3.22ff.; Luke 11.14ff.), in which the independence of Jesus from the recognized channels of authority leads some of the contemporary religious groups to suspect that his miraculous powers showed the influence of the powers of darkness. His opponents considered that, because Jesus was not recognized as an authoritative teacher, his power could not have been from God.

2 Early Christian table fellowship

Less than twenty years after the death of Jesus, Jews and pagans in a city in Syria were eating together on a regular basis. Some Jews in that context relaxed the rules that had hitherto maintained their identity. Perhaps there was a history of such eating together among Jews in Antioch as members of a minority culture sought to maintain social intercourse with men and women who did not share their faith. Whatever may have been the antecedents, in Antioch in the 40s CE experience of God and of others who claimed to be followers of Jesus led those men and women to new patterns of behaviour that were at odds with what most of their co-religionists practised. Paul describes the behaviour of those Christians in Antioch in his letter to the Galatians, when he stood up in defence of them to his fellow Church leaders (including Peter) who had suddenly got cold feet about their participation in this kind of table fellowship. It was an activity that seemed scandalous to more conservative elements in the Church. Representations were sent from the church in Jerusalem, imploring Paul and these newly established communities to desist from what might have appeared to some people to be 'unscriptural' behaviour.

It is clear from the passion with which Paul writes his letter that standing up to those who did not want to rock the boat was crucial for him. There was something important about the gospel practice that was in danger of being sacrificed by the attempt to try to be in continuity with the past. Paul had little or no basis in scripture for the kind of common table that he was supporting, in which Jews and pagans ate their meals together. Nevertheless his decision to support and encourage this kind of mixed dining and the practice of shared fellowship was absolutely central to what he understood his faith to be about. In his first letter to the Corinthians (Chapter 11), he reproaches those Christians in Corinth who would cause division, this time on class lines rather than on ethnic lines, and stresses the unity of the community in the one Spirit (1 Corinthians 12.13).

In this dispute, and in many of Paul's discussions about the Bible, Paul's opponents had all the best arguments, for they had both precedent and scripture on their side. Take the case of Abraham. Paul picks on Abraham's 'justification by faith' in Genesis 15.6 as an example of the way in which God justifies the ungodly without obedience to the Law. What he omits, however, is that just two chapters later the Bible mentions that God instructed Abraham to circumcise himself and his sons (Genesis 17.11–14, 23–24, 21.4). Paul, the rabbi, must have been aware of this. Though he had some grounds for his argument in the scriptures, they were nothing like as strong as his opponents' scriptural backing.

Nevertheless, despite this, Paul was persuaded that the experience of God of those pagans who had converted to Christ corresponded to what he and other Jewish Christians had experienced, and they enjoyed the authentic mark of God's presence without resort to the preservation of ancestral customs. What mattered most was that something that was in continuity with Christ was being done in their midst, not that the past was being preserved. Jews and pagans who followed Christ could leave behind aspects of the ancestral scriptures and live in different kinds of communities, with different norms of behaviour, based on conformity to Christ, which still managed to exhibit the fundamentals of love of God and neighbour, whatever they ate. In so doing they left Judaism behind, however much the Christians might have liked to think that what they were doing was in continuity with Jewish tradition.

3 Cornelius and clean food

There is something similar going on in the story told about Peter's journey to Cornelius in the Acts of the Apostles. As a result of his ecstatic experience, when he saw the sheet descending from heaven, full of unclean animals, Peter, a pious Jew, was persuaded to different attitudes towards non-Jews and to changed behaviour. The instruction in his vision to 'sacrifice and eat' cut across the very heart of his ancestral laws which, the Acts story tells us, Peter had kept. Yet this experience was confirmed by the witness of the conversion of the Roman centurion Cornelius without first converting to Judaism. Peter, we are told, believed that the same God was at work in these pagan converts as had been at work in the first Christians. So, as he puts it, 'if God gave them the same gift as he gave us, who believed in the Lord Jesus Christ, who was I to think that I could oppose God?' (Acts 11.17).

Now it is true that as Luke tells this story Peter feels in some sense duty bound to report back to the Jerusalem church about what went on. Historically, this kind of activity may have gone on occasionally, but the likelihood is that the attempts of the Jerusalem church to maintain oversight of the expansion and character of the emerging Christian movement was doomed to failure. Although Paul seems to have been part of a compromise solution about the obligations that new non-Jewish converts to

Christianity might have been expected to have accepted (Acts 15), there is not much to suggest from the Pauline letters that he insisted on this consistently with those who became Christians. Indeed, 1 Corinthians 8 has Paul allowing for a much more relaxed position with regard to the issue of meat sacrificed to idols than was allowed for in some versions of the decree that went out from the Jerusalem council (doubts about the exact wording of which are evident in the textual tradition about it (Acts 15.20)). Even allowing for Peter's willingness to be subservient to the consensus opinion of the elders in Jerusalem, the significance of what is described here is that nothing was ruled out as being impossible, and new developments could be countenanced and were not ruled out in advance.

Peter and Paul prioritizing experience of the Spirit

In the examples given above, what both Peter and Paul were doing was relativizing the place of scripture and tradition in the light of the present experience of the Spirit, who would 'guide them into all truth' (John 16.13); in Paul's case this occurred amid the new habits of life in the Antioch community, in Peter's case through an extraordinary visionary experience then confirmed by the dramatic conversion of a pagan soldier. In each case scripture had to be viewed afresh, with its meaning determined in the light of the experience of the love of Christ and the obvious marks of God's presence in the lives of those who, according to the law, should be outsiders. In doing this, Paul and Peter offered an approach to their ancestral scriptures which should be central to debate about the nature of Christian hermeneutics.

The place of the Bible in discipleship

These examples are helpful in thinking about the place of the Bible in Christian discipleship. They suggest that the prime Christian commitment is not to be obedient to the words in scripture, but to follow Christ and, in Paul's phrase, 'to be found in him' (Philippians 3.9). Of course, this still involves engaging with the Bible, for one comes to know about Christ by attending to what others have written about him. However, the Bible does not offer extractable 'answers' to modern-day questions, but rather lived examples of interpretation in action; that is, a record of the hermeneutical methods that Jesus, Paul, Peter and others deployed in the specific human situations in which they found themselves. Seen in this light, the New Testament writings point us to a form of Christian commitment that never bids us look to texts from the past as the prime source of understanding of the divine will, for that understanding is always to be found in Christ through the Spirit. The scriptures may be the vehicle of the divine Spirit, but Christ must never exclusively be bound to them. That view reflects a widespread conviction, with a long history in Christian theology and rooted in the Bible itself, that the prime responsibility of a Christian is to find Christ outside, rather than primarily inside, the pages of scripture.

Christianity not a religion of the book

For the reasons laid out above, in those places and times when Christianity has become a religion of the book, it has found itself at odds with its own foundation documents. However comforting the appeal to precedent or a written text might be, there is in Christianity's own foundation texts the story of a movement which, when it came to the crunch, was prepared to prioritize patterns of life conforming to their experience of Christ over ancestral custom.

Paul, perhaps above all others, ruined the notion that Christianity was a religion that could use the Bible as if it were a law code. The point could not be more tersely made than in his second letter to the Corinthians in which Paul writes, 'the letter kills, the Spirit gives life'. Paul pioneered an approach to the Bible of his own day (what Christians would now call the Old Testament), therefore, which might also apply to those of us who now look back on his words preserved in the scripture we now call the New Testament. According to his own hermeneutic, we should not be concentrating on the letter of Paul's words, but trying to get to their underlying point, to discern how they might help us – at a different time and place – to be imitators of Christ.

Paul appeals to the Corinthians to be 'imitators of me as I am of Christ' (1 Corinthians 11.1), yet this is not mere imitation of what Jesus did in Galilee and Jerusalem. Few Christians would want to practise exorcisms as Jesus did (according to the Gospels), even if we too would want to engage with the powers of evil, whether personal or social, in our own way and for our own time. What we are struggling to understand and embody are the contours of the *character* of Christ, as Philippians 2.6–11 indicates. We cannot know what this is just by appealing to scripture or tradition, though we will want to be aware of it.

New Testament meaning found in a human, not in words

This 'imitation of Christ' looks for the meaning of the words of the New Testament to be fulfilled in human lives in the same way that the New Testament looks back to the Jewish scriptures as texts, as words, whose meaning is likewise only completed or revealed in a human person: Jesus. Nowhere is this better stated than in the opening words of the letter to the Hebrews (1.1): 'Long ago God spoke to our ancestors in many and various ways by the prophets, but in these last days he has spoken to us by a Son.' God's 'speaking' is more through lives lived than words spoken or written. Christians lose sight of this when they treat the Bible as 'the word of God' rather than – in T. S. Eliot's phrase – 'the report of the Word of God'. This important distinction was addressed by the influential twentieth-century systematic theologian, Karl Barth. Barth stressed the importance of distinguishing between the words of the Bible and the divine Word in Jesus Christ to which the words of the Bible bore witness. He warned that there was a great danger in confusing the two as this would lead to God's revelation – which actually took place in a person and in the events of history – being confused with a book. When the record of human events comes to be seen as the revelation (rather than the events themselves being the revelation), the Bible can slip from being a resource of the Spirit towards becoming an instrument of power and oppression.

The Windsor Report: The Anglican Church responds to homosexuality

This major challenge to a legalistic use of the Bible from a writer (Barth) who has become a lodestone for conservative theologians is significant. Perhaps more surprisingly, it is echoed by the writers of the Windsor Report, the 2004 document which sought to offer a way forward in the debate over same-sex relationships within the Anglican clergy. Given the directness with which many Anglicans (particularly those of an evangelical orientation) have spoken on this issue, one might anticipate that their arguments are grounded in a blunt and legalistic hermeneutic in the Windsor Report itself. This is not, however, the case, as for much of that report, the Anglican Church suggests an understanding of scripture that is very similar in its hermeneutical structure to that of Barth:

> If the notion of scriptural authority is itself to be rooted in Scripture, and to be consonant with the central truths confessed by Christians from the earliest days, it must be seen that the purpose of Scripture is not simply to supply true information, nor just to prescribe in matters of belief and conduct, nor merely to act as a court of appeal, but to be part of the dynamic life of the Spirit through which God the Father is making the victory which was won by Jesus' death and resurrection operative within the world and in and through human beings. Scripture is thus part of the means by which God directs the

Church in its mission, energises it for that task, and shapes and unites it so that it may be both equipped for this work and itself part of the message.

How then does Scripture function in this way? . . . The early Christians understood themselves to be both beneficiaries and agents of the saving sovereignty of God, the 'kingdom' which had been accomplished in Jesus Christ. The 'authority' of the apostles . . . was their God-given and Spirit-driven vocation as witnesses of the resurrection . . . It is within this context of apostolic witness . . . that the writings we call the New Testament came to be written, precisely to be vehicles of the Spirit's work in energising the Church in its mission and shaping it in the holiness of new creation . . . From the first, the New Testament was intended as, and perceived to be, not a repository of various suggestions for developing one's private spirituality, but as the collection of books through which the Spirit who was working so powerfully through the apostles would develop and continue that work in the churches. This is why, from very early in the Church, the apostolic writings were read during worship, as part of both the Church's praise to God for his mighty acts and of the Church's drawing fresh strength from God for mission and holiness. This, rather than a quasi-legal process of 'appeal', is the primary and dynamic context within which the short-hand phrase 'authority of scripture' finds its deepest meaning.[1]

This is very much the open-ended, Spirit-oriented collaborative model of understanding that we advocate in this book. Hermeneutically (and this qualification is important as we have no sympathy with the kinds of ecclesial restrictions suggested later in the document) we share much with this part of the Windsor Report, as with Barth. None of us (including Barth, the Windsor Report and Wright) is advocating a legalistic appeal to scripture. All of us are advancing a hermeneutic that seeks to understand Christian discipleship within a larger theological context of which the Bible is a component part. What differs is the same issue that arose with regard to Tom Wright in Chapter 1: what should that larger context be? For Barth, Wright and the authors of the Windsor Report, that larger context is hierarchically structured and determined by the past such that interpretation is delivered from 'above', from 'tradition', whereby 'tradition' is understood as a monolithic framework for thought and action of the sort discussed in Chapter 1. The model we advocate – the model that we see operating in the examples from early Christianity discussed above – looks past this hierarchical hermeneutic, and seeks to find ongoing, contingent understandings of Christianity within the messiness and compromised 'sinfulness' of everyday life.

To reiterate the argument made in Chapter 1, the hermeneutic of the Windsor Report and of Tom Wright appears to be open-ended in principle, but retreats and is closed in practice. It's as if neither Wright nor the Windsor Report have the courage of their (hermeneutical) convictions. We wish to keep the hermeneutic that they propose open-ended, and argue that to do so is consistent with the practice of Jesus and the early Church: as the examples we have discussed in this chapter indicate, the appeal to 'what the Bible says' is what Paul so emphatically opposes, for he would point us to what a loving God is doing in transforming and enabling lives in the present through the Spirit. This will depend not on the letter of the text, but on using the Bible as part of the complex way of discerning what the divine Spirit is now saying to the churches.

The role of the Spirit

Too often Christians have ended up functioning as if they did not have a doctrine of the Spirit, or, if they have, somehow the voice of the Spirit is identified with the text of scripture or what Christians have said in the past (more accurately, what the majority of – and most influential – Christian voices have said). To take seriously the fact that 'the letter kills, but the Spirit gives life' (2 Corinthians 3.6) means quite simply that God's Spirit may be saying something new in speaking to our ever-changing situations. When writing to the Corinthians, Paul stressed how important it was to enable the Spirit to speak and inform the life of the Christian community. That could never be identified with the words of scripture, and, as he reminded them in 1 Corinthians 2.10–16, there is a profound interaction between the human and divine Spirit as the search goes on for discernment of the way of discipleship:

> [A]s it is written, 'What no eye has seen, nor ear heard, nor the human heart conceived, what God has prepared for those who love him' – these things God has revealed to us through the Spirit; for the Spirit searches everything, even the depths of God. For what human being knows what is truly human except the human spirit that is within? So also no one comprehends what is truly God's except the Spirit of God. Now we have received not the spirit of the world, but the Spirit that is from God, so that we may understand the gifts bestowed on us by God. And we speak of these things in words not taught by human wisdom but taught by the Spirit, interpreting spiritual things to those who are spiritual. Those who are unspiritual do not receive the gifts of God's Spirit, for they are foolishness to them, and they are unable to understand them because they are spiritually discerned. Those who are spiritual discern all things, and they are themselves subject to no one else's scrutiny. 'For who has known the mind of the Lord so as to instruct him?' But we have the mind of Christ. (1 Corinthians 2.10–16)

This remarkable passage indicates Paul's basic conviction, echoed elsewhere in passages such as Romans 8, that the divine Spirit enables a person to discern the way of God. The sentiments evident in this passage contrast with the unease that Paul expresses elsewhere in this letter about the way in which the Corinthians part company with him and the consequent reproof he offers them. Nevertheless, even if Paul believes that all who are spiritual will agree with him, the implication of 1 Corinthians 2 is that the indwelling Spirit in the life of the community will enable the individual to plumb the hidden truths of God. In such a situation the best that can be done is first to acknowledge the way in which all may be guided by the Spirit of God; second, to set forth the example of Christ (as, for example, it is acted out in the life of his apostle Paul); and third, to make charity the basic criterion of life together until that which is perfect comes (1 Corinthians 13.12).

The task of discernment

The ability of humans to get things wrong cannot be gainsaid, nor should this chapter be seen as subscribing to the naive view that modern people are somehow more enlightened than their forebears. We should attend to what our ancestors in the faith have said (all of them, including those whose voices are ignored, not just those whom the mainstream churches choose to hear and who are regarded as the mainstays of tradition). The risk of making a mistake should not short-circuit the patient quest to be attentive to the Spirit. One of the disasters for Christianity, from the first century to today, is the ease with which Christians have pressed the panic button in the face of deep disagreement, and the way they have anathematized dissent and behaved in ways that are in flagrant contradiction to the primacy of charity, 'the very bond of peace and of all virtues', as the collect puts it. The real possibility that we may err in our judgements of what the Spirit is saying to us neither absolves us of the difficult task of discernment – a collective enterprise if ever there was one – nor excuses us from facing up to the possibility that Christians in the past may have erred. They did about slavery and the role of women, to take just two examples. It is at least a question worth asking whether they may not also have done so in relation to same-sex relationships.

The collective nature of discernment is fundamental. In 1 Corinthians Paul spends a considerable amount of effort seeking to elucidate how one goes about maximizing community participation in decision-making. In 1 Corinthians 14, for example, he sets out a pattern of communal responsiveness to the Spirit, in which the different gifts contribute to the building up of the whole community. This process has to take place before understanding can come. The requirement for this to take place is the absence of the boasting, self-assertiveness and spiritual narcissism in which the Corinthian community abounds. No one has the right to boast, and all need to be attentive to one other so that the love about which Paul writes in 1 Corinthians 13 can come forth as the community, in faith and hope, seeks to move towards that time when God will be all in all.

In summary

The approach offered in this chapter is a reading of the biblical text in the light of what we, as modern interpreters, consider to be its essential subject matter. This has meant trying to get at the light of the truth of the Gospels even when that truth comes into conflict with the odd word or phrase. We shall see in a later chapter that this is an example of what is known as 'Sachkritik'. In providing this reading we offer a different hermeneutical model for consideration. We have focused on particular themes to interpret the whole of the Pauline letters, such as the unity of Jew and gentile in Christ, the importance of mutual love, and the concern for building up rather than strife. That judgement, of course, is contestable, and is a contribution to an ongoing debate among people who deeply disagree about a range of issues.

The point of this chapter, then, is not to offer an apologia for gay and lesbian relationships. Rather, we suggest that what we need to do is share experiences of seeking to live life in service to Christ, to recognize our differences, and *together* to be in the quest of truth, rather than assuming that we already know what this is. After all, it is Christ alone who is that truth, and at most scripture may bear witness to that truth. We can (and should) go to the New Testament, primarily the Gospels, as part of the process of discerning what it is that the Spirit points us to.

Now, as then, Christians are found deeply divided. In dealing with their divisions they should not stop talking with one another, nor should they anathematize those with whom they disagree. There will be deeply held convictions on both sides. Nevertheless, we shall not resolve the differences this side of the last judgement. Meanwhile, we 'see in a glass darkly' and only then, in that eschatological future, will see 'face to face' (1 Corinthians 13.10). Paul's own struggles to deal with massive differences of opinion and practice among the diverse groups to which he wrote offers us a model for reflection here. His advice to the Christians in Rome, for example, about how they should approach deep divisions in their community, is a salutary reminder that there is a different and better way than the pattern of mutual recrimination and anathematization to which Christians down the centuries have all too readily resorted. It deserves to be remembered in an age where too many of us think that we are the sole inheritors of the truth (Romans 14.1–4).

3

Interpretation in context

The conservatism of Christianity

One of the curious things about mainstream Christianity is how innately conservative it has become down the centuries. It is a backward-looking religion preoccupied with its sacred books and traditions. This applies to both Protestant and Catholic traditions, the principal difference between them being the relative weight they give to tradition and the Bible. The conservative nature of Christianity is so familiar that it no longer strikes us as odd. Why should it? It should, because the maintenance of traditional values and gender relations, and the endorsement of obedience to institutions like state, marriage and the family all sit uneasily with a religion whose founder seemed to be at best indifferent, or hostile, to them. In this regard, the real puzzle is why those who maintain orthodoxy pay such scant regard to Jesus.[1]

It is not that there is nothing in the New Testament that supports 'traditional values', but as many New Testament scholars have pointed out, the preponderance of evidence concerning such issues tends to come from books that are hardly mainstream in the New Testament as a whole, such as the Pastoral Epistles (probably not written by Paul) or 1 Peter, though there are occasional nods in a more conservative direction in the indubitably authentic letters, 1 Corinthians 14.34 being a good example. The heart of New Testament religion is not about maintenance of Judaism in another guise even if, historically, this is roughly speaking what Christianity became in the second century and later. As Chapter 2 showed, the New Testament writers themselves sat loose to the ancestral scriptures of Judaism and placed more weight on the Spirit.

How, then, has this state of affairs come to pass? There is no simple answer, but in this chapter we consider how certain forms of exegesis have, historically, become dominant and have thereby naturalized interpretive modes that consistently return conservative 'answers' from a set of Gospels that are essentially a profoundly radical set of texts. In order to do this we give an overview of dominant strands in the history of interpretation from the patristic, medieval, reformation and modern (post-Enlightenment) periods. We open out the question of whether 'interpretation' and 'application' of the biblical texts can (or should) really be separate activities, and in doing so develop the explorations of interpretation and context and of Sachkritik touched on in Chapter 2. We consider the widespread academic and ecclesiastical suspicion of contextual theology, and conclude by reflecting on the possibilities of critical interpretation, and on how important self-awareness is in this context. We begin, however, with the fundamentals: the basis of all interpretation, the literal meaning of the text.

Literal exegesis

Exegesis is the translation, interpretation, explanation and exposition of the Bible's various books. The literal exegesis of scripture is indispensable as without it we could not begin to discern what the signs on the page might mean. To understand the words of scripture they first need to be connected to a wider linguistic context (relating the Greek of the Gospel of Mark to the Koine Greek of the majority of the Greco-Roman world, for example) and the text can then be rendered in a modern-day language such as English. That is a significant enterprise in which the basic interpretive demands to begin to make sense of a text are set out: consultation of the best manuscripts and accurate construal and translation of passages in the original enable a reader to know what the text actually says and means. However, literal exegesis of scripture is in fact a limited enterprise as the task of understanding a text's meaning almost always moves beyond the literal in its recourse to analogies, such as parallels from other texts (whether inside or outside the Bible), and in its use of historical reconstruction. As a result, literal interpretation has never stood on its own, for in order for it to 'work' and its application to be made relevant to readers in situations different from those of the original writers, it has always been necessary to adopt additional interpretive methods.

No Christian literalist interpretation exists in isolation from other methods of interpretation. Even so-called 'fundamentalist' interpretation has worked with a sophisticated hermeneutic either by a form of dispensationalism (in which specific texts apply to specific periods of salvation history), or by a prioritizing structure (in which certain texts are subordinated to others in a hermeneutical hierarchy). In short, even a 'literal meaning' is always dependent on a supplementary context to ground it. This is the case even within the Bible itself, in which the 'literal' sense is rarely the only meaning – and often not even the foundational meaning – of a given passage. Consider, for example, the parable of the sower in Matthew 13.1–23: the disciples grasp the literal meaning of the narrative (a story about a farmer), but recognize that this is not the point. In response they not only press Jesus for an explanation – feeling the difficulty that we all share in interpretation – but also bemoan the fact that he speaks in metaphors at all. Sometimes, as in this case, they get an explanation, but that does not end the difficulties as the Bible not only enjoins us to make decisions about the interplay of types of meaning (literal, metaphorical, analogical and so on), but also presents the challenge of how we will connect these meanings to our lives. It is this challenge that is foregrounded on the many occasions when Jesus' interlocutor – whether Pharisee, Sadducee, rich young ruler or lawyer – asks him not about the *meaning* of the Law, but about its application to life.

Patristic and medieval exegesis

For most of its history the interpretation of the Bible was part of the life of faith. That is not to suggest that it was an uncritical activity, but that there was a widespread recognition that the interpretation of scripture was not engaged in as an end in itself but for the purpose of hearing God addressing the Church and also the individual. A variety of interpretive techniques contributed to the fulfilment of this goal, so that even the most apparently inhospitable parts of scripture could provide a means whereby the believer could be addressed by God. This approach is exemplified by Augustine in *De Doctrina Christiana* (397–?426):

> The student who fears God earnestly seeks his will in the Holy Scriptures. Holiness makes him gentle, so that he does not revel in controversy; a knowledge of languages protects him from uncertainty over unfamiliar words and phrases, and a knowledge of certain essential things protects him from ignorance of the significance and detail of what is used by way of imagery. Thus equipped, and with the assistance of reliable texts derived from manuscripts with careful attention to the need for emendation, he should now approach the task of analysing and resolving the ambiguities of the scriptures. When in the literal usages that make scripture ambiguous, we must first of all make sure that we have not punctuated or articulated the passage incorrectly. Once close consideration has revealed that it is uncertain how a passage should be punctuated and articulated, we must consult the rule of faith, as it is perceived through the plainer passages of the Scriptures and the authority of the church.[2]

Augustine wants accurately understood texts whose ambiguity is clarified through the 'plainer passages' of the Bible. The interpreter needs skill in language, and should go about his or her task in fear of God and under the authority of the Church. Clearly, for Augustine, establishing the meaning of biblical texts depends on a whole range of factors beyond just the literal meaning of the text itself.

Reformation exegesis: The 'literal sense' of scripture and the turn to history

In the patristic and medieval phases of biblical interpretation the main strands of doctrine and ethics were set out, and we find exegesis oscillating between the contrasting approaches of literal exegesis and allegorical ways of interpreting the Bible. This was accompanied by ongoing debate about the relative weight to be given to the literal sense of scripture as opposed to more imaginative or allegorical readings. At the Reformation, by contrast, there was a distinct preference for the 'plain sense' of scripture in preference to the manifold senses, which had been worked out in medieval exegesis drawing largely on the work of the patristic period.

Within Protestantism, scripture moved from being one important component in discerning the divine will to become the very foundation of Christian life and thought. During the Reformation and the Enlightenment this move towards the plain sense of scripture and the growing interest in history was political as much as theological because it was all part of a resistance to authoritative texts and institutions (such as the Church and the Bible). In this way, the literal sense – viewed as the meaning of the text in its supposed historical context – became the focus of interpretation.

Modern exegesis: The historical method since the eighteenth century

Following in the footsteps of the Reformers of the sixteenth century, most modern biblical exegetes consider the quest for the literal sense of scripture to be the essential task of exegesis. In the modern period this task has been linked with the elucidation of the historical context of biblical texts as the crucial determinant of their meaning. This has meant that a model of interpretation based on the received wisdom of the Christian tradition through time came to be replaced with a form of interpretation which either sat loose to that tradition of interpretation or rejected it completely. The academic biblical exegesis that has emerged in its place involves the patient attempt to attend to the words of the Bible in their original historical context, offering analogies by way of vocabulary and ideas from documents roughly contemporary with the Bible. The primary purpose is to ask what the author intended to mean by the text, and the secondary purpose is to determine how it would have been understood by its original audience. The process is intended to allow the text to speak on its own terms, and to avoid the temptation of hastily applying the text to the modern world.

'Exegesis' and 'application'

The emergence of the historical method as the dominant mode of biblical interpretation in the university and then the Church meant that there was a significant break following the Enlightenment with earlier patterns of interpretation. In this book we are not concerned primarily with a distinction between ancient and modern forms of exegesis, but with what we find to be a more useful distinction between those methods of interpretation in which scripture is one component in discerning the guidance of the Spirit, and those in which the meaning of the Bible is considered to be static and can be established by reference to a system that lies beyond the text – usually either 'tradition' or 'history'. This distinction presents a recapitulation of the two positions described in the last chapter (of 'open' and 'closed' hermeneutics) played out in the history of exegesis itself. To reiterate, those who seek to ground the meaning of the Bible objectively in a concept of tradition or history regard exegesis as something that can take place above and beyond particular human situations. Exegesis thereby becomes a transcendent act that takes place before 'application' of the Bible to specific life situations. Thus for many biblical exegetes the essential prerequisite *before* the exegete embarks on contemporary application is understanding, a distinction set out in an influential essay by Krister Stendahl.[3]

Exegesis as actualization

This distinction of exegesis from application is by no means a given. The distinction between 'pure' and 'applied' exegesis is one that has been subjected to critical scrutiny by Nicholas Lash. In two seminal articles Lash challenges what he calls the 'baton exchange' method of theological enquiry, in which the exegetes do their job and then pass their wisdom on to the systematic theologians and the ethicists.[4] More importantly, Lash challenges the notions that exegetes are free of philosophical and hermeneutical prejudices and are not themselves part of a tradition. Lash suggests that scripture is something to be performed, lived and acted upon and not just analysed. It is akin to the wealth of methods of scriptural interpretation explored in earlier centuries in the life of the Church touched on in Chapter 2. Interpretation means an 'actualizing' of the scripture (to use the term suggested in the Pontifical Biblical Commission's document of 1993),[5] in which understanding of the text comes in the process of living the texts. This is the position we advocate in this book, that interpretation needs to be situated in context, not from a position sitting over and above life. Liberation Theology, which we address in the next chapter, is a more radical example of contextual interpretation, and we look at others later in this book. First, however, we consider the advocacy of this method from two much more conservative sources: Karl Barth and the Pontifical Biblical Commission.

1 Barth's commentary on Romans

Karl Barth's implicit advocacy of contextual theology comes in his commentary on Paul's letter to the Romans, one of the most remarkable commentaries on the Bible from the twentieth or indeed any other century. In the preface to the second edition of the commentary Barth provides a lucid exposition of the nature of biblical exegesis, in which the relationship between ancient text and modern context is explained and understood in a way that encapsulates much of what we are trying to do in this book, capturing the subtle interplay between biblical text and the context of the reader. Barth notes the procedures of literal exegesis, which involve 'a reconstruction of the text, a rendering of the Greek words and phrases by their precise equivalents, a number of additional notes in which archaeological and philological material is gathered together', and argues that 'to press beyond this preliminary work to an understanding of Paul . . . involves more than a repetition in Greek or German of what Paul says: it involves the reconsideration of what is set out in the Epistle, until the actual meaning of it is disclosed.'

Barth's role model here is Calvin, about whom he writes:

> [H]ow energetically Calvin, having first established what stands in the text, sets himself to re-think the whole material and to wrestle with it, till the walls which separate the sixteenth century from the first become transparent! Paul speaks, and the man of the sixteenth century hears. The conversation between the original record and the reader moves round the subject matter, until a distinction between yesterday and today becomes impossible.

And this is the very model of interpretation that Barth himself is advocating:

> The matter contained in the text cannot be released save by a creative straining of the sinews, by a relentless elastic application of the 'dialectical' method . . . The Word ought to be exposed in the words. Intelligent comment means that I am driven on till I stand with nothing before me but the enigma of the matter; till the document seems hardly to exist as a document; till I have almost forgotten that I am not its author; till I know the author so well that I allow him to speak in my name and am even able to speak in his name myself.[6]

37

Barth here grasps something that is crucial to the exegetical task, namely the wrestling (however that may be done) in such a way that the biblical text and the interpreter can merge, dissolving the separation of exegesis and application in the process. His commentary represents a sincere attempt to discover what the text has to say, which is certainly pervaded with theological learning, but without the inhibitions of the norms of historical exegesis.

Sachkritik[7]

The task Barth sets out on here is called 'Sachkritik', a word not easily translated into English. It is about getting at the reality of the text, not merely by repeating or expounding its literal sense but by seeking to put into words what a biblical writer like Paul would be saying if he were here now. Later writers like Rudolf Bultmann suggested that Sachkritik was about correcting what Paul actually said (for example on homosexual practice) in terms of what he meant (the inclusiveness of the gospel), which might mean criticizing some of Paul's statements in the light of a broader understanding of the truth of the gospel, as understood by the modern interpreter's own wrestling with the scriptures. This is the form of Sachkritik mentioned in the previous chapter, which involves interpreting particular words or phrases and the scope of a particular idea in the light of the overall context. The origins of this approach lie deep within the New Testament, and are exemplified in the attempts by both Jesus and Paul to show what the Law of Moses is *really* about in passages like Matthew 22.36–40 and Romans 13.9–10.

The task of getting inside a text is ultimately not confined to the scholar or the clergy, for anyone can, at least in principle, offer insight as to what the text is really about, which (as we will see in Chapter 4) is something that Liberation Theologians have always maintained about the peculiar insight of the poor and marginalized. This method enables a space to open up for an imaginative relationship with one's own time and place, and for the work of the Spirit in a complex process of engagement with the text in which the subjectivity of the interpreter has a part to play.

2 *The Pontifical Biblical Commission*

A similar model of interpretation is provided in a document which, whatever its shortcomings, succeeds in grasping the fact that exegesis of the Bible is not just a matter of historical reconstruction or textual elucidation, because 'proper understanding of biblical texts is only granted to the person who has an affinity with what that text is saying on the basis of life experience'.[8] The Pontifical Biblical Commission underlines the importance of Sachkritik when it affirms:

> [E]xegesis is truly faithful to proper intention of biblical texts when it goes not only to the heart of their formulation to find the reality of faith there expressed but also seeks to link this reality to the experience of faith in our present world.[9]

> Reason alone cannot fully comprehend the account of the events of salvation. Faith lived in ecclesial community and in the light of the Spirit control its interpretation. As the reader matures in the life of the Spirit, so there grows also a capacity to understand the realities of which the Bible speaks.[10]

> Exegesis produces the best results when it is carried out in the context of the living faith of the Christian community, which is directed toward the salvation of the entire world.[11]

Here the Pontifical Biblical Commission, like the Windsor Report, like Barth, like Tom Wright, makes an explicit commitment to a Spirit-oriented contextual theology. However, that 'context' – in each of these cases – seems limited to the academic or ecclesiastical context within which they operate. There is little sense of 'context' here meaning 'life' in the way that most people think of that term. By contrast, Liberation Theology (a life-oriented contextual theology) is entirely dependent upon the conviction that the divine Spirit's work will emerge in the very process of commitment to, and practical concern and advocacy for, the vulnerable. It is significant that such examples of contextual theology have also been the most problematic for both academic and conservative theologians: many academic theologians consider contextual interpretation to be missing the boat, and the Catholic Church itself has rounded on Liberation Theology. To take one example, the Liberation Theologian Jon Sobrino has recently been reproached by the Vatican, and the 'faithful' have been warned about his teaching.

Modern suspicion of contextual interpretation

John Ashton gives a clear picture of the scholarly consensus concerning interpretation of biblical texts, and captures perfectly their associated treatment of those (such as Liberation Theologians) who wish to connect the text to 'life'. Ashton writes:

> [T]he old distinction between *meaning* and *meaning for* must be upheld. Feminists and liberationists, and any whose programme is based on or prompted by current ethical concerns – whether or not these have a direct biblical input – may be perfectly entitled to seek for further inspiration and encouragement in the Bible itself. They will have their own agenda and will usually, no doubt, focus their attention upon texts they think likely to yield some dividends, by way of inspiration or argument, to the cause they are eager to promote. But in so doing they should not pretend that they are attempting to *understand* the biblical text. Provided that they declare their interest openly, having already decided what they wish to find in the text (resembling the majority of Christian readers in the pre-critical era), then they may go their own way without fear of being disturbed by any of the findings of traditional exegesis. The two tracks may be parallel but they will never converge.[12]

Ashton is effectively saying, while all readers will want to do all they can to use the biblical texts merely as a peg on which to hang their own prejudices – what kind of understanding is that?

The protest of historical critics that they are interested only in what the text says (not what use it can be) is a necessary corrective to a self-indulgent kind of interpretation when *my* concerns are at the centre of the stage and the reading of the text is only there to confirm my prejudices. Positively, there is in this position a warning that needs to be heeded by all readers: the ongoing temptation to find in the text what suits us is enormous. There is not, however, a simple distinction (as Lash showed) between these two forms of theology. They actually share a great deal and the claims to disinterestedness and objectivity on the part of academic exegetes are by no means as clear as they might first appear to be. In the remainder of this chapter we first look at the dependency of biblical scholarship on such unscholarly things as imagination, and then move on to consider how all the exegetical methods we've discussed share a common goal of being critical, and what this might entail.

Imagination and modern exegesis

The key question is whether the historical approach was ever scientific or objective in the first place. This is a necessary question about the work of biblical scholarship as it puts a finger on the pulse of what actually gives modern exegesis its power: the way modern exegesis uses imaginative reconstruction as a means of enabling engagement with what are often obscure texts. Much has been written on questions of method and the 'scientific' character of historical exegesis, but the brute fact is that when it comes to the Bible, the historical sources contemporary with the Bible cannot bear the weight of the edifice of historical contextualization that is constructed upon them. No one doubts the extent of the material from the ancient world, nor the ingenuity of those who have used this to good effect in attempting to throw light on the Bible, but one should be realistic about the ability to write the kind of history that would be familiar to historians of other (particularly more recent) periods as the quantity of source material is just not available. Historical reconstruction goes on, it is true, but via the exercise of an extraordinarily imaginative juxtaposition of biblical texts with other sources in order to produce a narrative of their origins, functions and original contexts. Modern scholarship may seem to have moved towards a much more 'factual' or 'object-ive' engagement with the Bible, but this should not obscure the fact that it actually represents an extraordinary enterprise of collaborative imagination.

The hypothetical contexts that scholarly ingenuity has been able to offer have made many texts come alive. Raymond Brown's study of the Johannine literature, *The Community of the Beloved Disciple*,[13] for example, is a great read, but one should not sup-pose that the phenomenal knowledge of secondary literature means that we are any closer to knowing how the Gospel of John actually emerged and why it is such a different kind of text from the other three canonical Gospels. These questions stand as major unsolved problems of New Testament study, notwithstanding the enormous industry that has gone on to understand these texts historically. In short, modern academic exegesis is not only rigorously scholarly, it's also highly imaginative and even allegorical,[14] and it therefore shares with its intellectual prede-cessors more than at first appears.

The common goal of reading critically

None of us – Wright, Ashton, the Lambeth Commission – wants an arbitrary or entirely subjective approach to scripture; all of us wish to establish an appropriate critical approach to the biblical text. Where we differ is in our estimation of what a 'critical awareness' should involve. For Augustine, for example, a critical approach requires faith and an adherence to tradition, whereas for Ashton, a critical approach means a disinterested and scholarly historical contextualization of the biblical text.[15] In them we find critical methods articulated which reflect their different cultures of origin and traditions of interpretation. Augustine stresses the importance of the received wisdom of reading as part of a tradition, while Ashton represents the Enlightenment position characterized by the determination to read the Bible like any other text from antiquity, where under-standing the biblical text means allowing the text to 'speak for itself' without the concerns of the present day interfering with the exegesis of the text.

Critical self-awareness in exegesis

All of us read from within specific contexts, and by attending to those contexts (in the act of interpretation itself) we have the possibility of maintaining some awareness of our own prejudices which may condition or distort reading. It is here that contextual theology in all its various forms has stimulated dis-cussion and emphasized the need for attention to *where* reading is done and the effect of text on the interpreter and vice versa. Contextual theology offers a greater opportunity for interpret-ation to be self-aware than do the alternatives. It is the sort of self-awareness, by analogy, that comes in psychotherapy, and that can prevent us from perpetually re-enacting the errors or unhappiness of the past. The psychoanalytic tradition provides a helpful analogy here due to its focus on self-aware patterns of reflection, which enable the extent and character of power-relations to be ever-present as the quest for understanding goes on. Critical reflection involves some kind of process of distancing, to enable space for self-examination, and even for attention to the extent to which there is resistance to a text or too ready acceptance of its contents on the part of the reader.

That quest for understanding God's will, as we have argued throughout this chapter, is one that is rooted in practice and is not prior to it. In other words, the practice is itself the necessary context in which the understanding is developed and articulated even if the intellectual reflection and theorizing is a necessary complement. What is crucial about this is that critical awareness has a component of *human* engagement, and the involvement in that is the means of exemplification of what the text might mean and the basis for understanding and reflection. It does not pretend to be disengaged, disembodied, disinterested: how we relate to texts, therefore, is not solely about detachment or bracketing out self-involvement but rather developing reflective patterns which can demonstrate to us how our interpretation works and how it might contribute to community formation.

The priority of communicative interpretation

It is a mark of critical interpretation that it manifests not only an awareness of its own approach to the text but also the understandable constraints that this method imposes, and the necessity of openness to understanding, and distinguishing itself from, other interpretive methods as both checks and as a stimulus to change. Openness to others and to otherness is at the heart of being critical and is at the same time the way to openness to God. Critical interpretation should, therefore, be a model of communicative interaction. Insofar as any interpretive position eschews proper dialogue with the contextual theologies that are such an important component of modern theology, it ignores a fundamental component of both Old and New Testaments.

Imaginative, contextual discipleship is at the heart of the life of any Christian community. Contemporary situations throw up opportunities to interpret experience and conduct through the lens of scripture and, most importantly, vice versa, to discern the meaning of scripture through the lens of experience. Scriptural texts, read analogically, illuminate everyday life. In this, action and commitment are the necessary contexts of discerning God in the midst of human existence.

4

Liberation Theology

———•◦•———

Solidarity with the marginalized

In Chapter 2 we looked at some hermeneutical strategies of Jesus and the early Church. We now want to discuss a more contextually specific aspect of Christian hermeneutics: solidarity with the marginalized. This is central to the New Testament because a text like the Gospel of Matthew is concerned not only with obedience to Jesus' words (though it is that), but with our responses to those who – like the executed Jesus himself – have found themselves outcast, vulnerable and destitute (e.g. Matthew 25.31–45). In this chapter we think about specific examples of the hermeneutical approaches advocated in the previous chapter which claim that God is not to be found in a tradition that stands over and above human situations, but rather to be found in those situations themselves. The justification for such an approach is everywhere in the Gospels. In the poignant words of the Son of Man in the story of the last judgement, for example, 'inasmuch as you have done it to one of the least of these you have done it to me' (Matthew 25.31–45). To put it another way, the Gospels themselves suggest that the quest for God's love, justice and holiness begins amid the struggle for human justice and compassion. It is from that position of solidarity that we are able to move to love of God, and from there back to love of our fellow humans.

The theology of the New Testament involves an understanding of faith from a position of real solidarity with all suffering and exploited people. It suggests that theology is not worked out in isolation from pressing human realities, for it is in those realities that the Spirit of God speaks to people and beckons them to find the way of God. Given this emphasis in the New Testament, it is astonishing that in all the countless words written about the importance of faithfulness to Bible and tradition the words and example of Jesus should feature so little. There are, of course, many exceptions, and this chapter deals with a major exception: Liberation Theology. Liberation Theology is a modern instance of the discernment of the call of God in everyday human experience: it is a hermeneutic in which experience and the insight of social context are given a prime place.

Liberation Theology: An overview

From the late 1960s, Brazil was in the grip of a military dictatorship. The Church found itself offering the only space for protest against the brutality and oppression of a regime that placed economic growth before the well-being of the millions of poor and marginalized. The Church was catapulted into a position of protest, offering a crucible for the birth of a new kind of community: this is the context in which Liberation Theology was born. The contrast between gross affluence of the tiny minority and squalor and poverty for the majority has prompted priests and those in religious orders to think again about their apostolic task, and in so doing they have learnt the importance of living and working with and learning from the poor. As a result, the theology of liberation has taken root outside the walls of the seminaries and the basilicas, often far away from the nearest priest.

Liberation Theology is a form of contextual theology in which the experience and circumstances of the interpreters are given prime importance as the first step in seeking to become disciples of Jesus. The approach is embodied in the popular education material familiar in the Latin American churches where the experience of poverty and oppression (often termed 'life' or 'reality') is treated as being as important to understanding (if not more so) as the text of scripture itself. 'Life' represents another text to be studied alongside that contained between the covers of the Bible. God's word, then, is to be found in the dialectic between the literary memory of the people of God (the Bible) and the continuing story of the people of God to be discerned in the contemporary world, particularly among those people with whom God has chosen to be identified. Carlos Mesters explains the interplay of these two 'texts' within Liberation Theology as follows:

> [T]he emphasis is not placed on the text's meaning in itself but rather on the meaning the text has for the people reading it . . . the common people are also eliminating the alleged 'neutrality' of scholarly exegesis . . . the common people are putting the Bible in its proper place, the place where God intended it to be. They are putting it in second place. Life takes first place! In so doing, the people are showing us the enormous importance of the Bible, and at the same time, its relative value – relative to life.[1]

Liberation Theology therefore arises out of the specific needs and concerns of the poor. There is no expectation that the Bible, the tradition, the theologians, or even the bishops, will offer unambiguous guidance independent of the circumstances in which the people of God find themselves. The basic theological assumption undergirding this approach is that God does not come from outside the situation of poverty and oppression but is to be found in and through that situation as much as in the Bible, church and tradition.

The place of Liberation Theology

Liberation Theology has been enabled and located among the poor of Brazil through CEBs (Communidades Eclesiais de Base). CEBs are basic ecclesial communities, the local communities in which the presence of Christ is to be found and the peace and justice that Christ came to offer is explored and reflected upon. CEBs represent a key aspect of mainstream Roman Catholic doctrine of the church, but in Liberation Theology they have become the arena in which local communities seek to explore their commitment to Jesus Christ through action for justice and peace. Here, then, is a modern example of the sort of open-ended, contingent, contextual hermeneutic which we advocated in the previous chapter, and saw examples of in the early Church in Chapter 2.

Significantly, Liberation Theology has strong (and powerful) opponents, and has met – in a Catholic context – with a similarly resistant hermeneutical logic to that embodied in the Windsor Report in its response to homosexual clergy. A long-standing opponent of Liberation Theology is the current pope, Joseph Alois Ratzinger. Ratzinger dislikes Liberation Theology because it has a hope for the redemption of this world. As an Augustinian, Ratzinger disbelieves in that redemption, for he considers that heaven – rather than a renewed earth – is the destiny of humans. The Liberation Theology project, by contrast, hangs on to the belief that God's kingdom comes on earth as in heaven, and it thereby propounds an eschatological vision at odds with that of Ratzinger and his authoritarian, hierarchical understanding of community.

Insofar as Roman Catholicism is hierarchical, the theology produced at the top of that hierarchy, and the life situations it serves, is very different from that at the bottom. The magnitude of that difference can be glimpsed in a written record of Liberation Theology in action, and offers an appropriate place to begin. This account describes the experience of James Pitt at São Paulo, Brazil in 1980:

> The theme of that fortnight was 'that Jesus was born poor and humble and shares our life,' and the question was 'Why?' The eight women present were all poor. None had much formal education. Most were migrants from rural areas. All knew real hardship. They could easily identify with a poor family on the move whose baby had been born in a stable. Indeed a one-minute reading of Luke's account of the Nativity provoked a one-hour

discussion of the injustices, humiliations, and hardships that the mothers themselves experienced.

They discussed the terrible health services available in the area and how a local woman's baby had been born while she was waiting in queue to see the doctor. (The baby died.) They swapped accounts of having to wait in shops while better dressed people were served first and how as domestic servants they were treated without respect by their mistresses. They talked of the high cost of food in the local shops. After an hour the catechist put the question, 'Why did Jesus choose to be born poor and humble?' 'Maybe,' said one woman, a mother of ten of whom three had died and only two were working, 'maybe it was to show these rich people that we are important too . . .'

A ripple of excitement went through the room. Was God really making such a clear statement about *their* humanity? About *their* rights as [persons]? The discussion progressed, but with an electric charge in the air. Half an hour later, a young woman said: 'I think we still haven't got the right answer to the first question.' A complete hush. 'I think,' she went on, 'that God chose his son to be born like the rest of us so that *we* can realize that we are important.'[2]

This brief example gives an indication of just how different the Bible, theology and Jesus himself can look from the situation of poverty.

The methodology of Liberation Theology

The first step of the theology of Liberation is to immerse oneself within the reality of the context in which one finds oneself: commitment precedes reflection in the understanding of injustice. The second step is theological in something approaching a traditional sense. It consists in confronting the reality of suffering, analysed and better understood in the light of the revelation learnt in the heart of the church community. Finally, there is an orienting reflection towards more insightful action. What is central is that the theology of liberation is done by those who are either directly involved in liberating action, or at least linked with it.

Among the CEBs, the Bible has become a catalyst for the exploration of pressing contemporary issues relevant to the community, and thereby offers a language so that the voiceless may be heard. There is an immediacy in the way in which the biblical text is used, as resonances are found between the experience of those in the community and those set out in the stories of biblical characters. Through this process the Bible offers a means by which the present difficulties can be shown to be surmountable in the life of faith and community commitment. The community setting also means an avoidance of narrowly individualist 'religious' readings.

Parables of Today: Biblical education in Brazil[3]

Enabling the poor to read the Bible has involved a programme of education about biblical material, such that it can be a resource for thousands who are illiterate. An example of this material is the educational packs known as 'Parables of Today', which were distributed by the archdiocese of São Paulo during the 1980s. Each pack contains a series of slide-sequences based on the parables of Jesus, but which relate stories told within the CEBs in São Paulo, Brazil. In the example below (see page 52), the parable of the lost sheep (Matthew 18.12–14) is told through a story about the arrest of a trade union activist. The slides come together with a commentary and suggestions for ways of using the material.

The material reflects the input from the distinguished educator, Paulo Freire (1921–97), whose influence on popular education throughout the world has been enormous. In his pedagogical writings Freire emphasizes the link between knowing and doing, experience and learning. He criticizes a view of education in which students become accumulators, storing material away as if in a banking process. In particular, Freire criticizes the roles played by teacher and student within the 'banking concept of education', in which the all-knowing teacher fills the grateful, ignorant and inert students with deposits of 'knowledge' concerning the roles of oppressor and oppressed. What Freire promotes instead is a process whereby human beings engage in active yet critical forms of education through which they embrace both their world and each other. Freire believes that education must be the site of transformation in which the traditional pupil–teacher relationship is dealt with, for this relationship maintains and mirrors other forms of oppression within society. Analogically, the ways in which one engages in theological education are inseparable from the questions that theology deals with. Thus the transformation of the learning process into a student-centred education is not a fashionable learning technique; it is central to the understanding of community power-relations, and engagement with those power-relations at the level of education is part of the commitment to a far more wide-ranging societal transformation.

The Freirean methodology is evident in the Brazilian material. Groups start with the short slide sequence which gets them in touch with the familiar scenes of everyday life in urban Brazil. This is necessary as many participants feel that the biblical text is far too sacred for them to interact with, whether critically or in relating it to everyday life. After viewing the slides, groups are asked to discuss the story and encouraged to recall similar experiences, identify with various members of the story, and share what their own feelings might have been. At another, later, meeting the relevant biblical text (the parable) is read and discussed and a comparison is made with the story in the slides in order to provoke discussion. It is only at the end of the process that a commentary consisting of a summary of recent scholarship on the parables is read and discussed along with the group's own insights (drawn from the experience) on the present call to discipleship in the community.

PARABLES OF TODAY

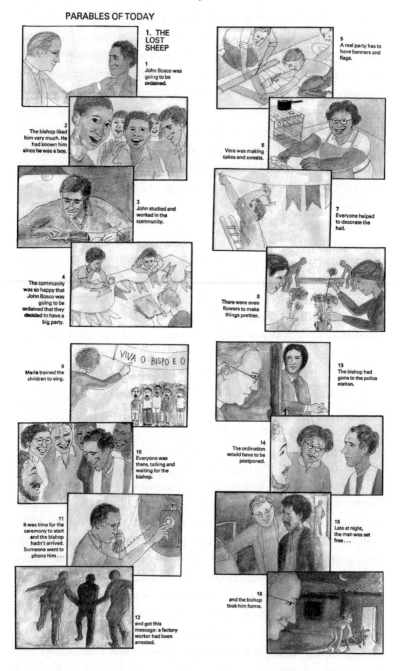

1. THE LOST SHEEP

1 John Bosco was going to be **ordained**.

2 The bishop liked him very much. He had known him since he was a boy.

3 John studied and worked in the community.

4 The community was so happy that John Bosco was going to be **ordained** that they **decided** to have a big party.

5 A real party has to have banners and flags.

6 Vera was making cakes and sweets.

7 Everyone helped to decorate the hall.

8 There were even flowers to make things prettier.

9 Maria trained the children to sing.

VIVA O BISPO E O

10 Everyone was there, talking and waiting for the bishop.

11 It was time for the ceremony to start and the bishop hadn't arrived. Someone went to phone him . . .

12 and got this message: a factory worker had been arrested.

13 The bishop had gone to the police station.

14 The ordination would have to be postponed.

15 Late at night, the man was set free . . .

16 and the bishop took him home.

Members of the group are asked to have three points in mind as they read: (1) a parable is an example that has only one idea, the rest are details to make the story interesting; (2) the parables speak of Jesus and of his mission; (3) Jesus preached the parables to make us think, to revise our way of seeing the world and to change our lives. In the concluding commentary it is stressed that the power of the community lies in its preoccupation with the needy and in its search for those who are lost and who most need the community's support:

> The community of God's people does not exist for itself. It was called by God to serve those who are lost, because they have no land, no job or no home, because they are hungry, sick or suffering persecution. So the parable shows that the model of the Church is not preserving the ninety-nine sheep who at the moment are gathered together. The model of the Church is to search unendingly for the needy. Mercy is at the centre of daily life. Jesus tells us that the Church that acts this way is imitating his ministry. Jesus was always criticised by the religious people of his time who thought that he should always be with Church people. But whenever Jesus met anyone who needed help, he always went to the needy and the poor. So Matthew thought that the Church of his time had forgotten this, as his community was too directed to its own needs. He told this parable to all but with special appeal to those responsible for the community: 'Be true pastors as Jesus was! Be missionaries! The search is urgent. Go now to those who need you the most!'[4]

We have used this particular sequence many times in educational events in the UK since returning from Brazil in 1983. Without exception the material has provoked a free-ranging, participative discussion. The most common reaction among British respondents is surprise at the juxtaposition of the story of the ordination with this particular parable as most people's reaction is to say, 'Isn't this parable about evangelism?' Also, many participants have reacted negatively to the gender stereotyping in the Brazilian story: the women bake the cakes and prepare the flowers; the union worker and the bishop are both men. But this, of course, reflects Brazilian reality. In a similar way we may feel ill at ease with the monarchical language and viciousness of the treatment meted out in some of Jesus' stories. Few of us can have failed to wince at the ending of the story of the unmerciful servant at the end of Matthew 18! In this respect, the parables of Jesus are just as context-related as the stories from Brazil, and they may not be immediately applicable to other cultural situations. Relating them to another situation therefore becomes part of the process of understanding the ways in which we bridge the hermeneutical divide between text and contemporary context.

Differences between Liberation Theology and academic theology

Liberation Theology has been a protest at the way theology can be disconnected from ordinary life. Its starting place was not detached reflection on scripture and tradition in a private library or cloistered rooms. It began amid the life of the shanty towns, the land struggles, the lack of basic amenities, the carelessness about the welfare of human persons, the death squads and the shattered lives of refugees. It began in a sub-continent which at the time of Liberation Theology's genesis was dominated by military dictatorships and vast discrepancies in wealth and life opportunities. For these reasons it is distinctively different from the theologies of North America and Europe, as theology needs to say something very different to the poor from what it might say to the rich. Gustavo Gutiérrez characterizes that difference in this way:

> [T]he question in Latin America will not be how to speak of God in a world come of age, but rather how to proclaim God as Father in a world that is inhuman. What can it mean to tell a non-person that he or she is God's child?[5]

Liberation Theology is above all a new way of *doing* theology, which holds that detachment and silent reflection are inadequate unless accompanied by action. In this respect it contrasts with much post-Enlightenment theology centred in universities and seminaries where the priority placed on intellectual discourse means that it is deemed a virtue for theology to be detached from life and, increasingly, from the practice of prayer and charity. What has been rediscovered in Liberation Theology is the commitment to the poor and the marginalized as a fundamental for the meeting with God. This commitment and solidarity are the necessary basis for theological activity. So, one first of all *does* Liberation Theology rather than learning about it. Liberation Theology cannot adequately be understood except by commitment in solidarity and action: this is an extension of Lash's argument that exegesis and application cannot be separated from each other.

Understanding involves the move from a position of detachment to one of involvement, in order to be open to that transformation of perspective that comes either at the margins or in social estrangement. To paraphrase the dialogue of Jesus with Nicodemus in John 3, it is only by changing sides and identifying with the Christ who meets and challenges men and women in the persons of the poor, the hungry and the naked that one may 'see the Kingdom of God' (cf. John 3.3). It is the commitment and active involvement with the poor as participants with them and recipients of their peculiar role in the order of the universe that is the basis of criticism. Liberation Theology, therefore, is not to be confused with some kind of armchair radicalism in which the thoughts of a liberal intelligentsia allow an Olympian perspective on the doings of fellow men and women. Indeed, it is precisely those doings, at least the lot of the most vulnerable and the weakest of the earth, that grant a different, critical, kind of perspective.

These theological presuppositions reflect crucial issues in the Bible. In Jeremiah 22.16, for example, the prophet asserts that knowing God comes through doing justice: 'He defended the cause of the poor and needy, and so all went well. Is that not what it means to know me? declares the LORD.' Likewise, in the

Gospels, the fundamental learning experience of the disciples is not so much the teaching of Jesus, but their activity in walking with him on the way to Jerusalem. The reported prophecies of the passion (e.g. Mark 8.31; 9.31; 10.33–34, 45) are incomprehensible without the learning experience of the way of the cross, which is not just a spiritual journey, but – as all the Gospels indicate – a political journey into the very teeth of Judean politics. Jesus becomes the victim of the high priest's decision that 'it is expedient for one man to die for the nation' (John 11.49). To learn what it means that the Son of Man must suffer means taking up the cross (Mark 8.38) and following Jesus by going up to Jerusalem.

Social hierarchy in the parables

Liberation Theology illuminates the relationship between hierarchy and hermeneutics. It does so by stressing that the perspective of the poor and the marginalized offers a different story, an alternative to that told by the wielders of economic power whose story becomes the 'normal' account. In the CEBs, hitherto oppressed persons have become the particular means whereby the divine perspective on human existence is offered. They are the 'little ones' who are vouchsafed a peculiar insight into the identity of the divine wisdom (Matthew 11.25). The vantage point of the poor is the vantage point of the crucified God and can act as a criterion for theological reflection, biblical exegesis and the life of the Church. The poor are the means whereby the Church can learn to discern the truth, direction and content of its mission and can assure itself of being the place where God is to be found.

For affluent western Christians, Liberation Theology raises really important issues about the ways in which we tame and domesticate biblical material: attending to the perspective of Liberation Theology gives us a self-awareness and a critical vantage point on our own interpretive practices of the sort advocated in the previous chapter. The model for this understanding through an inversion of hierarchy is central to the Gospels, and, taking our cue from the slide sequence discussed above, we now look at the inversion of hierarchy in the Bible, with specific relation to the example of the 'little ones' mentioned in Matthew. The 'little ones' – like the 'sinners' of our title – are nobodies, and should not, says the hierarchy, have a place in interpretation. In the light of the foregoing discussion we contest this, and argue that the reverse is true: the outcast and marginalized can have, in fact, a privileged form of insight (Matthew 11.25).

In Matthew, the parable of the lost sheep comes in the context of a discussion about humility and in response to a question from the disciples: 'Who is the greatest in the kingdom of heaven?' (Matthew 18.1). Jesus responds by offering children as a paradigm of the appropriate relationship of disciples to the kingdom (Matthew 18.3–4). In the ancient world, children were generally regarded as of little account; and yet, Jesus suggests, those who are like them in their insignificance are counted greatest in the kingdom of heaven.

Children and 'little ones' as representative disciples

In Matthew's Gospel, the response to the child or the 'little one' that is advocated is the same as the response advocated towards Jesus himself. Just as fulfilling the needs of the hungry and the thirsty in Matthew 25.31–45 means doing service to the heavenly Son of Man, so receiving a child means receiving Jesus. The position of children in the first century CE was greatly inferior to the more child-centred world of today. They were, as a matter of course, often treated, by our standards, brutally, although they were sometimes believed to be in close contact with the divine world by virtue of their marginality. In Matthew, where the child moves to centre-stage, these contrasts are evident. The child Jesus poses a threat to King Herod in Jerusalem in the opening narrative. Later it is children alone who greet the meek and lowly king as he enters Jerusalem (Matthew 21.15). In contrast, the hierarchy seeks to persuade Jesus to rebuke the children. To place a child in the midst of the disciples, then, is to challenge the assumption that the child has nothing of worth and can only be heeded when it has received another's wisdom. The implication is that the ordering of things that characterizes the adult world is not, after all, the embodiment of wisdom and may in fact be a perversion of it (themes characteristic of Freire, and, as we will see in Chapter 6, Blake).

In Luke's Gospel, the parable of the lost sheep is recounted in response to a charge made against Jesus that he received sinners and ate with them (15.1–7). The conclusion to this and the story of the woman and the lost coins (Luke 15.7 and 10: 'there will be joy in heaven over one sinner that repents'), together with the parable of the prodigal son, show that the focus of God's concern may not match our hierarchical standards. In Luke, Jesus offers the parable of the lost sheep in defence of his practice of ministering to outcasts (Luke 15.2). The story stresses joy in the recovery of that which was lost, and proclaims that this human joy is a picture of the joy of God over the sinner who repents. Similarly, in Matthew's narrative it is part of a warning to be attentive to the 'little ones'. To do the will of God one must not take lightly the loss of a single one of the flock, however insignificant. Despite the fact that most commentators on Matthew assume that the material in the Gospel was about church members (rather than about those considered to be insignificant), other passages in Matthew like 10.42 and 7.21f. blur the boundaries between insiders and outsiders. Jesus takes a child – not a *believing* child or a *good* child – and so uses that child and its experience as a model of discipleship.

So the neat solution commonly offered to the problem of the identity of the little ones, which confines them only to Christians, seems to be excluded by both the immediate and the wider context. There is an insistence throughout Matthew that only those who do the will of the Father in heaven will be admitted to the kingdom of heaven (Matthew 7.21–23). They, and only they, will be acknowledged by Jesus as his 'brother, and sister, and mother' (Matthew 12.50). Matthew's Gospel hardly allows its readers to remain content with a distinct delineation between those inside and outside the sphere of God's activity and concern. As the parable of the wheat and the tares (Matthew 13) makes plain, no one is in a position to sit back and make a clear assessment of those inside and outside the scope of God's (and therefore the community's) concerns, or to judge who is the greatest in the kingdom of heaven.

In summary

The understanding of the Christian scriptures is an activity and a discipline inseparable from what happens in this world, most especially to 'the least of these who are members of my family' (Matthew 25.40, NRSV). The welfare of all people is fundamental to the nuanced and complex business of the interpretation of texts and of living according to the Spirit of God in this world. Understanding of God's self-revelation in Jesus Christ comes through our resolve to do the will of God and through our capacity to extend our imaginative grasp of God's action in the world (John 7.14–24).

Two things are central to this model. First, this is not only about thought but also about action, about the lived lives of people seeking to embody the way of God in faithful struggle for justice. Second, this method (as Clodovis Boff has argued) does not presuppose the application of a set of principles or a theological programme or pattern to modern situations. We need not, then, look for formulas to 'copy' or techniques to 'apply' from scripture. What scripture offers us is rather something like orientations, models, types, directives, principles, inspirations: elements permitting us to acquire, on our own initiative, a 'hermeneutic competency' and thus the capacity to judge – on our own initiative, in our own right – 'according to the mind of Christ', or 'according to the Spirit', the new unpredictable situations with which we are continually confronted.

The Christian writings offer us, in Clodovis Boff's words, 'not a what but a how, a manner, a style, a spirit'.[6] Those words are important. What Boff wrote about the interpretation of the Bible applies just as much to the way in which Christians approach the whole of life. The two dimensions of interpretation, the text and its context, and the readers and their context, are both necessary.

Liberation Theology has been in the vanguard of criticism of a narrowly ancient historical concern in modern biblical interpretation. At the same time, Liberation Theology has itself been criticized for making the Bible conform to twentieth-century concerns. These criticisms are both important in terms of the possibilities of self-understanding and critical reading raised at the end of the previous chapter. Liberation exegesis shares with mainstream biblical study a concern to be critical, and western exegesis can thank the liberationist perspective for the incessant reminder of its own partiality.

5

Christian radicals:
Denck and Winstanley

Radical nature of early Christianity

Christianity started life as a radical movement within Judaism. It brought with it a reorganization of power relationships (both between men and women, and between different races) that marked a different ethos, an anticipation of a commonwealth that would eventually be operative throughout the universe. The earliest Christian writings bear witness to movements which, in the various facets of their social life, promoted the democratization of what had hitherto been elite privileges and values: holiness, knowledge, wealth and power. Those Christians who began to implement these deep-seated convictions in their daily lives were practitioners of the kingdom-life amid a political reality that seemed to militate against its fulfilment.

There is a dynamic of radicalism at the very heart of the New Testament, whatever conservative and cautious elements are to be found alongside it. Yet centuries of appeal to those reactionary forces in the face of movements of reform has obscured the steady flow of radical ideas throughout Christian history. Those radical ideas have so often appealed to the roots: to Jesus and the early Church as paradigms of what Christian polity and action should be about. They have frequently been articulated by those with a strong sense of prophetic vocation calling them to challenge received wisdom and practice. In the history of Christian radicalism the scriptures have offered a resource, but 'what the Spirit once said' has not been allowed to determine responses to what the Spirit now says to the churches in the present. These radical Christians have been less concerned with abstract reflection, and more with active engagement to see another kind of order at work in the world: God's kingdom on earth, and the discernment of God in the context of 'seeking first God's kingdom and God's justice' (Matthew 6.33).

Those who have sought to engage in radical change – whether thirteenth-century radical Franciscans, Anabaptists on the left wing of the Reformation, or twentieth-century theologians – know that the sacred texts themselves offer a warrant for their deeds and beliefs.[1] What is not sufficiently acknowledged is how deeply rooted (we would say *more* deeply rooted) in the New Testament they are than the rather narrow, censorious approach to religion that has come to typify Christianity. Some redress of the balance towards the wisdom of the 'radicals' is long overdue.

Radical use of scripture

Many radical Christian interpreters refuse to be content with the letter, but pierce to what they consider to be the real meaning of the text. This attitude may manifest itself as a rejection of the priority of scripture and a subordination of it to the inner understanding that comes through the Spirit. As in Liberation Theology, the meaning of scripture and tradition is subordinated to experience, as a prior 'text' which must be the necessary condition of the way in which scripture is read. There is a democratic, participative emphasis on the ability of all those open to the Spirit of God to understand the meaning of scripture. This can come without access to the wisdom of the experts. According to Acts 2, when Peter preached on the day of Pentecost it was about a promise of the Spirit being poured out on to 'all flesh', not just apostles: women as well as men, old as well as young, insiders as well as outsiders, would prophesy.

At the Reformation writers like Erasmus and Tyndale stressed the importance of enabling ordinary people to read the Bible and to reflect on the world in a way that enabled them to glimpse something of the way of God, to discern the divine way in the present, or – as some recent Brazilian popular educational material puts it – to enable one 'to look at the world with new eyes'. They viewed this text as one that spoke to people whether or not they had spent years studying it. As Chapter 4 showed, patterns of biblical exegesis that have emerged in parts of Latin America over the last thirty years offer a more recent example of the way in which the practical faith of the non-professional reader can be resourced by a mode of reading of the scriptures that does not need (even if it was often supported by) sympathetic intellectuals.[2]

It is this kind of knowledge of God through the practice of justice and compassion that we find in the writings of four very different men from four different centuries: Hans Denck in the sixteenth century, writing at the very beginning of the Reformation; Gerrard Winstanley in the seventeenth century, writing during the English Revolution; William Blake, writing and engraving in the eighteenth century during the French Revolution; and William Stringfellow in the twentieth century, writing amid the events of the Civil Rights movement and the Vietnam War. In this chapter and the next we give brief accounts of the inspirational lives and beliefs of these four exemplary Christian radicals.

Hans Denck (c. 1500–27)

Historical context

There can have been few more dramatic periods in European history in which to come to theological maturity than the 1520s, a moment when Europe was fracturing politically, socially, economically and theologically. In 1521 Luther was excommunicated by the Church of Rome; in 1524, fired by radical Reformation ideas, the Peasants' War began: a massive popular insurgency against the Holy Roman Empire, which spread from Germany into Austria and resulted in perhaps 100,000 deaths. Bubonic plague was on the move again in Switzerland, while in Henry VIII's England Tyndale began work on his English translation of the New Testament. This would eventually be published in Germany and subsequently at Antwerp, where, a decade later, Tyndale would be charged with heresy, then strangled and burnt at the stake. This was the world of Hans Denck, a young man who by 1527 was lying in a house in Basle, Switzerland, dying of the plague. Denck had profound theological insight, and had lived at the heart of contemporary events, yet because of his untimely death his influence on Reformation thought was insubstantial, and he has largely been overlooked in the history of Christian thought.

Denck's life

Denck was born in Upper Bavaria at some time close to the beginning of the sixteenth century. He had a wide-ranging education at the universities of Ingolstadt and subsequently Basle, where Erasmus – perhaps the most famous humanist scholar of the day – was teaching at the time. Denck's early career looked promising, he married, and became rector of St Sebald School in Nuremberg. His success, however, was short-lived as his understanding of Christian life did not accord with that of the authorities. Denck was what would come to be called an Anabaptist, as he had undergone rebaptism as a sign of his own commitment to Christ and his move to a new way of life in which violence was abhorred and attentiveness to the law of God, written on the heart, became the norm for Christian living.

Denck's theology

Denck believed that God dwells within all creatures, for all people have their origin in God. All people, even though they may not recognize it, have access to this inner experience of God, somewhat akin to what Paul describes in 1 Corinthians 2.10–16. To have access to this inner experience is to be guided by the Spirit, and that guidance was especially important, in Denck's view, to interpretation of the Bible. That Spirit is Christ, the Word, indwelling in the life of the individual, and Denck subordinates the words of scripture to the Word that is Christ: the importance of scripture lies not in itself, but in its witness to the Word that became flesh, Jesus Christ. Denck writes:

> Holy Scripture I hold above all human treasure but not as high as the Word of God that is living, powerful and eternal – unattached and free of all elements of this world; for since it is God himself, it is Spirit and not letter, written without pen or paper so that it can never be eradicated . . . Therefore, salvation is not bound to scripture however useful and good it might be in furthering it.[3]

Tradition of mysticism

Denck stands in the tradition of late German medieval mysticism, expressed in *Theologia Germanica*, a work which also influenced Luther. At the heart of his theology is the conviction that 'to be poor in Spirit' (Matthew 5.3) involves both humility and divinity. To understand scripture one must understand the spirituality to which the work of the divine Spirit within oneself bears witness. As one seeks the Truth one is assisted by the divine Word, whose success in the soul depends on the faith or dependence of the human soul. As Clarence Bauman so eloquently puts it, the one who 'exalts scripture above what it teaches, namely to love God with all one's heart, displaces content with form and educates himself like those scribes who were unfit for the Kingdom of God. Scripture is a letter the purpose of which is that we might know its author'.[4] Denck suggests that just as the disciples left all for Christ's sake and yet did not understand who he was until they had accompanied him on the Way, so the life of obedience is the way in which one knows him.

So, in Denck's view, it is the Spirit within each person that is necessary for the interpretation of the Bible: this is the primary means of knowledge of God to which the Bible itself is subordinate. In language that is remarkably close to that of late twentieth-century Liberation Theologians, Denck, echoing 1 John, stressed that 'none can truly know Christ except insofar as he follow him with his life'.[5] The centrality of Christ is all-important on this point, for the one 'who wishes to know and to attain true Love, cannot receive it more directly and more easily than through this Jesus Christ'.[6] Experience and understanding come together in Christ because being truly human means embodying Christ's love and self-giving in one's life. That can be comprehended and followed as the result of the truth already existing in human hearts. For Denck, therefore, much as in the letter of James Chapter 2 and 1 John 4.7–21, religion is the transformation of the individual and the good deeds that are the result.

Love the fulfilment of the law

Denck writes of the way of Christ as the fulfilment of the law, that is to say, love is the fulfilment of the law of Moses,[7] and it is in Christ that the 'law is fulfilled' (Romans 8.3). Christ's law of love is inscribed in the human heart and this is demonstrably fulfilled in the life of Christ which humans are called to share. Denck, then, has a concept of Christianity grounded in the law, but that law is located in the human heart where God dwells, rather than in an external institution or authority. For this reason Denck returns us here to the question of authority in interpretation which was raised in Chapter 1 and has been an ongoing theme throughout this book. Like many other radical Christians, Denck saw that scripture is not the possession of the experts, nor is it the kind of text that is transparently self-interpreting. Like Barth (whose views were discussed earlier), Denck gave priority to obedience to Christ the divine Word, over against the words of scripture.

Like so many who have looked inward for God's will, Denck was attacked by those who thought that God's love should be primarily embodied in, and policed by, ecclesiastical institutions. Nuremberg's city council was at this time reformist, and antagonistic to the principles of Anabaptism. By 1525 Denck's name became known to them and he was made to stand trial for his 'heretical' views. When the authorities could not extract a verbal response with which to condemn him, they forced him to write a 'recantation'. Denck was in a dangerous position – just two years later Felix Manz, a fellow Anabaptist, would be put to death by drowning in Zurich, the particular form of execution that the Zurich council saw fit for those rebaptized. In the event Denck was not executed, but was banished from Nuremberg and forced to leave his wife, family and possessions behind. He made his way to Strasbourg where again his 'heretical' views became known, and in 1526 he was banished from that city too.[8] Only a year later Denck, presumably worn down by the stress of these and other similar experiences, succumbed to the plague. He contributed little to the history of Anabaptism, but ideas like his filtered into non-conformist English religion at the beginning of the seventeenth century and became the religious soil out of which the Quakers and our next radical writer – Gerrard Winstanley – emerged.

Gerrard Winstanley (c. 1609–76)

If Denck came to maturity at a key moment of European religious history, Gerrard Winstanley did so at a key moment of English political history. Winstanley lived and acted a little over a century later than Denck in equally fraught and confrontational circumstances in a country whose identity was being profoundly reshaped. The year 1649 was astonishingly eventful in Britain: following almost a decade of civil war, Charles I was beheaded in January and England declared a commonwealth. The events that were taking place seemed so extraordinary – the termination, for example, of what had presented itself as a divinely ordained and permanent monarchy – that many people sought to read the signs of the times in biblical terms. Religion was inextricable from the progress of political events, and even within the ranks of the revolutionary Roundhead

New Model Army there were strong radical elements. Like Denck, Winstanley was risking his life by speaking out in the way that he did, and like Denck, Winstanley wanted to live out his theology in practice. It was a strange practice – initially indecipherable from the outside – for what Winstanley and others set about doing was digging the earth: cultivating common land for crops. It was a practice that only makes sense in the light of Winstanley's life and radical Christian outlook.

Winstanley's early life

There is little information about Winstanley's early life, but it appears to have been without dramatic event.[9] Born near Wigan, probably educated at a grammar school, Winstanley moved to London as an apprentice tailor, where he subsequently married and set up business trading textiles. The Civil War had a negative impact on his business, forcing him to close in 1643, and he moved to the countryside, twenty miles or so southwest of London where his father-in-law owned a property. Here he worked as a grazier, but this too ended in financial failure and depression. However, amid these ashes Winstanley experienced a spiritual rejuvenation and a period of prophetic inspiration beginning in 1648.

Winstanley's theology

Like Denck, Winstanley belongs to a long line of Christian radicals who have emphasized the ability of *all* people to understand the ways of God, and have stressed the importance of the Spirit in intellectual engagement, and of inspiration and experience alongside memory and what Winstanley calls 'book-learning'. Like many of his radical predecessors Winstanley also recognized the importance of visions as vehicles to discern the underlying state of things, and he engaged dynamically with the imagery of the books of Daniel and Revelation – particularly the references to the beasts arising from the sea – as a means to comprehending the oppressive political powers which kept the common people in thrall.[10]

The Fall

Winstanley's writings also display a sophisticated use of the Christian doctrine of the Fall. For Winstanley, the Fall meant that humans had turned towards a life of the flesh rather than of the Spirit, and that Fall was manifest in the possession of private property and the social inequalities that arise from it. The fallen world is ruled by 'men' of flesh who are corrupted by their greed, and consequently consider social inequality to be 'righteous':

> The man of the flesh, judges it a righteous thing, That some men that are cloathed with the objects of the earth, and so called rich men, whether it be got by right or wrong, should be Magistrates to rule over the poor; and that the poor should be servants nay rather slaves to the rich.[11]

Winstanley's theological hope is that this situation may be overcome through a restoration of humankind to the Spirit; that is, to the recognition of Christ living within individuals again. He therefore contrasts the fleshly 'man' with the Spiritual 'man', the latter being an individual who has a quite different vision of the world, grounded in justice and equality:

> But the Spiritual man, which is Christ, doth judge according to the light of equity and reason. That al man-kinde ought to have a quiet substance and freedome, to live upon earth; and that there shal be no bond-man nor begger in all his holy mountaine. Man-kinde was made to live in the freedome of the Spirit, not under the bondage of the flesh, though the lordly flesh hath got a power for a time, as I said before; for every one was made to be a Lord over the Creation of the Earth, Cattle, Fish, Fowl, Grasse, Trees, not any one to be a bond-slave and a beggar under the Creation of his own kinde. Gen. 1:28.[12]

As this use of Genesis suggests, Winstanley believed the earth to have been originally a 'common treasury' for all to share. The practice of buying and selling the land – which allowed some to become rich and others to starve – constitutes the Fall of Adam from which humanity, severally and corporately, stands

69

in need of redemption. The religious and political elements cannot be separated out here, as it is the presence of Christ – that is, the spiritual 'man' in the life of individuals – that will overthrow the corrupt regime of the fleshly man. The Spiritual democracy at the root of this vision means that the redemption of the earth will necessarily be a communal event:

> But this is not done by the hands of a few, or by unrighteous men, that would pul the tyrannical government out of other mens hands, and keep it in their own heart [hands] . . . But it is done by the universall spreading of the divine power, which is Christ in mankind making them all to act in one Spirit, and in and after one law of reason and equity . . .
>
> When this universall law of equity rises up in every man and woman, then none shall lay claim to any creature and say, *This is mine, and that is yours, This is my work, that is yours*; but every one shall put to their hands to till the earth, and bring up cattle, and the blessing of the earth shall be common to all . . . Act. 4:32.[13]

Winstanley's reference to Acts here is to a description of the early Church that would now be called 'communist': 'All the believers were one in heart and mind. No one claimed that any of his possessions was his own, but they shared everything they had.' Thus the vision of the restored earth is rooted, for Winstanley, in community rather than in capital:

> There shall be no buying nor selling, no fairs nor markets, but the whole earth shall be a common treasury for every man, for the earth is the Lords. And man kind thus drawn up to live and act in the Law of love, equity and onenesse, is but the great house wherein the Lord himself dwells, and every particular one a severall mansion: and as one Spirit of righteousness is common to all, so the earth and the blessings of the earth shall be common to all; for now all is but the Lord, and the Lord is all in all. Eph. 4.5, 6.[14]

Winstanley was effusive in the communication of this vision, and between 1648 and 1652 he wrote more than twenty politico-religious tracts. This would have been just another exercise in theological utopianism if Winstanley and others had not attempted to put it into practice. But they did. Winstanley and the 'Diggers' were convinced that a moment had come in history when the promises for God's kingdom on earth were about to be fulfilled, and on Sunday 1 April 1649 they went out to St George's Hill near Cobham and began to cultivate the common land there. In Davis and Alsop's words:

> They wanted to realize the aspirations set out in Winstanley's *The New Law of Righteousness* and to test the logic of the revolutionary events of early 1649 which rid England of kingly government and claimed to make the English a free people living in a free commonwealth.[15]

The Diggers saw themselves as agents of its coming at 'the acceptable time' (kairos) and sought to improve the lot of the hungry and landless through the cultivation of the common land to create the kind of society they believed had existed before the Fall. It is sadly predictable that their actions were met with fire and fist: the hostility of local landowners ensured no communities survived for long, driving the Diggers away with arson and physical violence.

Realized eschatology

Winstanley was an advocate of what one might term a 'realized eschatology' in which future hope is not only a possibility but also the very condition of the life he lived. His was a conviction, moreover, that the coming of the kingdom was dependent on human repentance rather than an inevitable and inexorable divine action (cf. Acts 3.19). The Second Coming takes the form of Christ 'rising up in sons and daughters'[16] and drawing them back into a Spirit of true community. The new heaven and earth is something to be seen here and now, for monarchical power is the old heaven and earth that must pass away. The New Jerusalem is not to be seen only after one dies: 'I know that the glory of the Lord shall be seen and known within creation, and the blessing shall spread within all nations.'[17] As with Denck, God is not far above the heavens, but is to be found in the lives and experiences of ordinary men and women. As in Liberation Theology, Winstanley sees that the restoration of the earth is indivisible from the spiritual restoration of humanity. Now, more than ever, this is a timely message, given our downward spiral into environmental apocalypse.

6

Christian radicals: Blake and Stringfellow

William Blake (1757–1827)

In 1794 France was ablaze with revolution. Robespierre was leading the French people into the Reign of Terror, guillotining thousands of civilians. Frightened English politicians looked across the Channel at the carnage and began to implement a series of repressive measures at home to ensure that the revolution did not spread to Britain. Meanwhile prophets and artists, particularly in London, were interpreting events – just as they had in Winstanley's day – in terms of the apocalyptic visions of the book of Revelation. Living in London at the centre of events, the engraver, artist and poet William Blake composed and printed prophetic books from his home in Lambeth. Despite his recognition now as one of the greatest poets and engravers of his day, Blake was largely unknown during his lifetime. Significantly, he is still by and large ignored by the theological community to whom he has most to offer. For Blake is another Christian radical, who – like those we saw in the previous chapter – saw through the fissures in his fragmenting culture the possibilities of a new kind of human life.

'The Garden of Love'

'The Garden of Love' is a poem from *Songs of Innocence and of Experience*, a collection Blake produced and published in 1794. The image (see p. 74) depicts a sort of religious education, the priest reading and gesturing, the two children, heads bowed,

listening attentively, but also uncomfortably. Looking more closely at the picture, it is apparent that as the priest reads from (presumably) the Bible, he gestures and directs the adolescent children towards the grave. The picture suggests that the religion the priest preaches is one of death. Why death? The age of the children is significant here: as the poem makes clear, this is a work about how sexuality, death and morality are linked together by the Church. The adolescent children are a boy and girl, on the edge of 'experience' (like Adam and Eve), and the nature of their sexuality – at least how it's being set out by the priest – is represented symbolically in the image: the male and female genitals hinted at by, respectively, the phallic gravestone to the right of the priest and the open grave before him. Sexuality – in the eyes of religion – is sinful, mortal, deathly.

The poem reads:

> I went to the Garden of Love,
> And saw what I never had seen:
> A Chapel was built in the midst,
> Where I used to play on the green.
>
> And the gates of this Chapel were shut,
> And 'Thou shalt not' writ over the door;
> So I turn'd to the Garden of Love,
> That so many sweet flowers bore,
>
> And I saw it was filled with graves,
> And tomb-stones where flowers should be:

And Priests in black gowns were walking their rounds,
And binding with briars my joys & desires.[1]

The poem and the engraving do not illustrate each other so much as present different perspectives on a common theme. In the poem, a scene of love has been dominated by an inaccessible chapel while all around graves have taken the place of flowers: the symbols of life have been transformed into the symbols of death. The poem is about the impact of a 'thou shalt not' religious mentality when simply 'applied' (here by the priest) to human lives, and in this case, the subject of human love. As a hermeneutical critique, it could stand as an image of an Anglican bishop reading the Windsor Report to Gene Robinson and Jeffrey John.

Blake's context

This poem doesn't deal with the Bible itself, but rather looks to the use to which the Bible and 'Christianity' are being put in Blake's society. Blake is not dealing with specific doctrinal points or acts of the Church, but is considering the way in which pernicious structures of thought are unthinkingly circulated as 'religion', and what the impact of that circulation might be on human minds and lives. For these reasons, Blake presents the 'Christianity' of his culture not as a social movement enacting the Spirit-oriented life advocated in the Gospels, but as an institutionally oriented tyranny that co-opts the Bible to sustain its own ends. The 'religious' in Blake's culture constitute a status quo concerned primarily with the maintenance of existing power structures and hierarchies. Blake is therefore concerned with our complicity in systems in which religion becomes both ideological (the embodiment of a set of largely unconscious ideas) and hegemonic (dominant within its particular social structure). 'The Garden of Love' speaks to this situation precisely because there's no space for reflection or questioning in the poem. The chapel has simply been 'built in the midst'; there's no meaningful relationship between the chapel and the garden – between religion and love – but rather one of colonization or occupation. The human corollary of this is the priest and the children whose relationship shows how ideology is indoctrinated and internalized (presumably under the name of 'what the Bible says' or 'what God wants').

We considered in earlier chapters how Christianity has gained momentum as a conservative movement, and how it has rather lost sight of Jesus and the early Church as it has done so. Blake is unusually articulate on this topic, and he has a disconcerting ability to make visible the gap between Jesus and 'Christianity'. Like William Stringfellow, as we will see later in this chapter, Blake is able to put his finger on the 'powers and principalities' that govern society, and like Winstanley he is able to relate the ways in which context affects interpretation, or why it is that 'The man of the flesh, judges it a righteous thing . . . that the poor should be . . . slaves to the rich.' This can make Blake uncomfortably incisive: as T. S. Eliot put it, 'He was naked, and saw man naked, and from the centre of his own crystal . . . He approached everything with a mind unclouded by current opinions. There was nothing of the superior person about him. This makes him terrifying.'[2]

Blake's work is not limited to the sort of critique that he offers in poems such as 'The Garden of Love'. That critical aspect of his work exists alongside a positive articulation of alternative ways of engaging with the Bible, of understanding what 'Christianity' might mean and how a critical – and in this case artistic – encounter with 'tradition' can reveal new forms of understanding.

Spirit essential to interpretation of the Bible

Like others whom we have discussed in previous chapters, Blake thought that Christianity is not a religion of the book, but that the Bible is just one component of Christian life, and that it only has a meaningful role when read in the light of the Spirit. He wrote:

> The Bible or \<Peculiar\> Word of God, [when read] exclusive
> of conscience or the Word of God Universal, is that Abomina-
> tion which like the Jewish ceremonies is for ever removed &
> henceforth every man may converse with God & be a King
> & Priest in his own house.[3]

In other words, if the Bible is read without reference to
('exclusive of') conscience or the 'Word of God Universal' (i.e.
Christ), it is, in Blake's view, an abomination. It corresponds,
for Blake, to the 'abomination' of ceremonial religion that
Jesus removed. Jesus, as the incarnate God, brought God and
humanity together in a relationship that no longer needed
to be mediated by state religion, hence Blake's comment that
'henceforth every man may converse with God & be a King &
Priest in his own house'.

Blake recognized that the Bible, divorced from conscience,
read as a dead letter, all too easily becomes a monolith, particularly when it gets into the hands of the powerful. Blake
considered this monolithic, hegemonic Bible to have been the
justification used for much of the inequality and exploitation
that was all around him. At the end of the eighteenth century
he saw a national Church in collusion with the state that
sanctified itself through appeal to that biblical monolith, and
disregarded the miseries of the poor. In this self-perpetuating
system, the Bible is used to ground tradition, and tradition used
to interpret the Bible. It is a cycle of justification, in Blake's view,
grounded in ideas of morality and law.

Blake's contemporaries read Bible as moral law

The central problem, in Blake's view, with his contemporaries'
reading of the Bible was that they interpreted it as a book of
moral law (the 'stony law', as he calls it). In doing so, the focus
of their religious lives became moral uprightness, and the ongoing legalistic appeal to the Bible made it into a reference work,
a rulebook, a manual of morals. In Blake's view, this form of

Christianity is indivisible from the moral judgement of one another. This is evident in 'The Garden of Love', where 'religion' is embodied in and constituted by the repressive morality that it inculcates. Blake takes this contemporary model of Christianity back to the Bible and shows how incompatible it is with the Gospels. He shows that in the Gospels this preoccupation with moral law is identified with the scribes, and he argues that when we judge one another, we take on the role of the accuser, which is, in biblical terms, the role of Satan (see e.g. Job 1.6). Blake thinks the conflict between Jesus and the scribes arises precisely because Jesus comes to replace a religion of judgement (which blocks relationships between people) with one of compassion (which opens us to the experience of God in one another). Jesus offers the paradigm of how moral idolatry can be overcome through his ministry of the forgiveness of sins. The forgiveness of sins means a relinquishment of the barriers of judgement that block relationships between people, and it reopens the possibility of collaborative hermeneutics.

Forgiveness of sins – morality is not Christianity

For these reasons, Blake sees forgiveness – rather than morality – as the central concept of Christianity and he never tires of arguing that Jesus brings the former, not the latter: 'If morality was Christianity, Socrates was the Saviour. The Gospel is Forgiveness of Sins & has no moral precepts – these belong to Plato & Seneca & Nero'.[4] And again:

> There is not one moral virtue that Jesus inculcated but Plato & Cicero did Inculcate before him. What then did Christ Inculcate? Forgiveness of Sins. This alone is the Gospel & this is the Life & Immortality brought to light by Jesus. Even the Covenant of Jehovah, which is this: 'If you forgive one another your trespasses so shall Jehovah forgive you [so] that he himself may dwell among you. But if you avenge, you murder the Divine Image & he cannot dwell among you [and] because you murder him he arises again & you deny that he is arisen & are blind to Spirit.'[5]

When we live in that spirit of mutual love and forgiveness, God lives in us, and we in him. For Blake (who argues that 'God is Jesus'), Jesus reveals the true or full nature of God:

> Jehovah's Salvation
> Is without Money & without Price, in the Continual
> Forgiveness of Sins,
> In the Perpetual Mutual Sacrifice in Great Eternity! for
> behold!
> There is none that liveth & Sinneth not![6]

Forgiveness is qualitatively different from Law, Blake believes, because it cannot be codified in a book. This is exemplified by Jesus' response when Peter seeks to establish the limits of forgiveness: 'Then Peter came to Jesus and asked, "Lord, how many times shall I forgive my brother when he sins against me? Up to seven times?" Jesus answered, "I tell you, not seven times, but seventy-seven times"' (Matthew 18.21–22). There is a clear contrast here with the law of retaliation: 'if there is serious injury, you are to take life for life, eye for eye, tooth for tooth, hand for hand, foot for foot, burn for burn, wound for wound, bruise for bruise' (Exodus 21.23–25). Unlike retaliation, forgiveness cannot be quantified, and is always particular to each life situation. Forgiveness of sins means an openness to the Spirit such that we're always in the business of negotiating a way forward based on mutuality rather than exclusion.

Imagination

Blake has a name for this open-ended way of relating to the Bible and to one another through forgiveness and creativity: he calls it 'the Imagination'. We have touched on the theme of 'imagination' earlier in this book. 'Imagination' has many different meanings ('the faculty or action of forming new ideas, or images or concepts of external objects not present to the senses': *New Oxford English Dictionary*). Blake uses the term to point to a kind of thinking that is qualitatively different from what might be termed 'legalistic' thinking. There are many forms of legalistic religion that provide a model of Christianity that is about following inflexible rules. But being open to the Spirit means having to improvise, to engage attentively in new situations. 'Imagination', therefore, is one way of describing a non-legalistic way of interpreting. For Blake it represents humanized law, life in Christ. He expresses this relationship by explicitly identifying the Imagination as 'the Divine Body'. In other words, the Imagination – open-ended, Spirit-oriented interrelating – is what brings all people together in the body of Christ.

Blake and the Bible

These factors give Blake an interesting vantage point on the Bible, which he regards as an open-ended imaginative resource through which we may gain understanding, and not as a book of moral law. One might think that there is an inherent difficulty for this view given that the Bible often, and explicitly, presents itself as a book of moral judgements. Moreover, these judgements can sometimes seem to valorize the vengeful, the underhand, the proud and the violent. To a casual observer Samson, for example, seems to have little moral function in the book of Judges beyond being God's tool for slaying Philistines. This, however, is grist to Blake's mill. The fact that the Bible contradicts itself, tells the same narrative in different ways, and contests its own interpretation (for example, in Jesus' rereading of the Law and Prophets) makes it an open-ended text. For Blake this differentiates it from the manifold branches of human knowledge – such as science, theology and philosophy – that seek an internally consistent and hermetically sealed structure of thought.

Blake recognized that while the Bible bears witness to the Word of God, it contains many other elements as well, which have often been used to condone injustice. Blake was indignant about this, wishing to return the Bible to its role as an emancipating text rather than its current position as the textbook of tyrants. He therefore feels no compunction to attempt to make the Bible internally consistent or universally benevolent, and he embraces the 'problematic' elements within the Bible as a means to question dominant readings of the Bible within his own culture. So, while there can be few writers and artists whose work is so permeated with biblical themes, Blake is at the same time one of the Bible's fiercest critics. For example, Blake probes the fissures in the depiction of God as a remote monarch and lawgiver in the Bible as a means to challenge dominant readings of the Bible of his own day that promulgated patriarchy and authoritarianism. This biblical critique is, moreover, delivered through an astonishingly diverse array of poems, engravings and paintings that make Blake simultaneously both England's greatest 'Christian' artist, and also its most radical biblical interpreter.

William Stringfellow (1929–85)

'I walked up and saw these guys doing strange things. They were doing it three ways. One: They were setting fire to the hootches [houses] and huts and waiting for people to come out and then shooting them up. Two: They were going into the hootches and shooting them up. Three: They were gathering people in groups and shooting them.

'As I walked in, you could see piles of people all through the village . . . They were gathered up into large groups.

'I saw them shoot an M-79 [grenade launcher] into a group of people who were still alive. But it [the shooting] was mostly done with a machine gun. They were shooting women and children just like anybody else.

'We met no resistance and I only saw three captured weapons. We had no casualties. It was just like any other Vietnamese village – old Papa-san, women and kids. As a matter of fact, I don't remember seeing one military-age male in the entire place, dead or alive. The only prisoner I saw was about 50.'[7]

This is the first-hand account of Sgt Michael Bernhardt, who on 16 March 1968 was serving in a platoon in Vietnam. The US soldiers killed up to five hundred civilians that day: babies, children, women, the elderly. In Bernhardt's words, 'The whole thing was so deliberate. It was point-blank murder and I was standing there watching it.' But point-blank murder was not only taking place in Vietnam – back in the US, events in the civil rights movement were coming to a head. On 4 April, less than three weeks after the My Lai massacre, Martin Luther King was shot dead in a motel in Memphis.

How does theology speak to these situations? Is this the world in which theology lives? If the Bible really connects to modern life, shouldn't it have had something to say about the institutionalized racism that the civil rights movement was confronting, and about the foreign policy that put the US in Vietnam, as it – with the UK – is now in Iraq? William Stringfellow believed it did, and that the 'powers and principalities' mentioned in Ephesians 6.12 and elsewhere corresponded to the forces of death at work within his own time and place, the USA. For this reason, Stringfellow saw the My Lai massacre not as an aberration by an otherwise benevolent nation, but as an exposure of the true nature of the forces of death governing US society. Stringfellow would later write: 'My Lai is no aberration but a direct implementation of the euphemistically stated strategic intent.'[8]

There's nothing unusual about 'left wing' interpretations of governmental activities with a Christian twist. The power and authenticity of Stringfellow came from the fact that the connection between world and religion that he preached wasn't itself disembodied: he practised what he preached and lived his religion.

After a privileged education – a scholarship at the London School of Economics and a degree at Harvard Law School interspersed by three years' service in the US army – Stringfellow had all sorts of lucrative and agreeable options open to him. His decision, however, was to practise law in the depressed district of Harlem, offering services to those who others – for either financial or aesthetic reasons – wouldn't touch. More importantly, he did this not from a comfortable place, but from its centre, choosing to live among those he served. Martin Luther

King, himself from a middle-class background, moved into a Chicago slum tenement in 1966 in order to draw attention to, and gain an understanding of, that poverty. Stringfellow, in exactly the sort of engaged act of solidarity that we saw enacted by Liberation Theology in Chapter 4, did the same thing, not as an experiment but on a permanent basis. He writes here about his new 'home' in Harlem:

> The stairway smelled of piss.
>
> The smells inside the tenement – number 18, 342 East 100th Street, Manhattan – were somewhat more ambiguous. They were a suffocating mixture of rotting food, rancid mattresses, dead rodents, dirt, and the stale odors of human life.
>
> This was to be home. It had been home before: for a family of eight – five kids, three adults. Some of their belongings had been left behind. Some of their life had, too.
>
> The place, altogether, was about 25 × 12 feet, with a wall separating the kitchen section from the rest. In the kitchen was a bathtub, a tiny, rusty sink, a refrigerator that didn't work, and an ancient gas range. In one corner was a toilet with a bowl without a seat. Water dripped perpetually from the box above the bowl. The other room was filled with beds: two double-decker military cots, and a big ugly convertible sofa. There wasn't room for anything else. The walls and ceilings were mostly holes and patches and peeling paint, sheltering legions of cockroaches.
>
> This was to be my home.
>
> I wondered, for a moment, why.
>
> Then I remembered that this is the sort of place in which most people live, in most of the world, for most of the time. This or something worse.
>
> Then I was home.[9]

From this place he worked with the disowned and dispossessed, in a predominately black and Hispanic subculture marked by poverty and lack of access to basic services.

In *An Ethic for Christians and Other Aliens in a Strange Land*, Stringfellow seeks 'to treat the nation within the tradition of biblical politics – to understand America biblically – not the other way round, not (to put it in an appropriately awkward way) to construe the Bible Americanly'.[10] At the heart of his method is the conviction that the Bible, and particularly the Apocalypse, can assist one to understand a particular moment of time because it enables an enhanced vision of the reality that confronts one.[11] For Stringfellow, the Apocalypse does not offer a time-table about the end of the world but a template by which one can assess the theological character of the world in which one lives.

Stringfellow does not expect to go to the scriptures as if to a self-help manual that offers off-the-shelf solutions. Nor is he interested in abstract principles or grand theories to apply to human situations. For him the ethics of biblical people concern events not moral propositions: 'Precedent and parable, not propositions or principle'.[12] There is no norm, no ideal, no grandiose principle from which hypothetical, preconceived or carefully worked out answers can be derived because there are no disincarnate issues: all issues are incarnate in the phenomena, events, people and institutions of this world. The Apocalypse's stark contrasts offer an interpretive key to understand the cosmos under God and the situation of his nation in the 1960s, 1970s and early 1980s. Stringfellow followed in a long and distinguished tradition in which Babylon and Jerusalem are types of two different kinds of religious community. Babylon is a description of every city, an allegory of the condition of death which is the focus of apocalyptic judgement. Jerusalem is about the emancipation of human life in society from the rule of death. The Apocalypse is a parable, he said, of the church of prophecy, an anticipation of the end of time.[13]

Stringfellow's work has many affinities with Latin American Liberation Theology, particularly as it is reflected in the life of the CEBs. He explored those areas of life in action where one is confronted with the limits of compromise: what to protest about and what to keep quiet about, how to act prophetically, and how to avoid just taking the line of least resistance. For him there was a need to emphasize the particularities of every situation through an ongoing, contextualizing task for which there are no simple answers from the scriptures. Biblical theology does not deduce 'the will of God' for political involvement or social action, and the ethics of biblical politics give no basis for divining specific, unambiguous, narrow or ordained solutions for any social issue. The Bible does not yield 'right' or 'good' or 'true' or 'ultimate' answers in seemingly private or personal matters, and even less can it be said to do so in political or institutional life:

> The impotence of any scheme of ethics boasting answers of ultimate connotation or asserting the will of God is that time and history are not truly respected as the context of decision making. Instead, they are treated in an abstract, fragmented, selective, or otherwise, arbitrary version hung together at most under some illusory rubric of 'progress' or 'effectiveness' or 'success'. From a biblical vantage point as much as from an empirical outlook, this means a drastic incapacity to cope with history as the saga in which death as a moral power claims sovereignty over human beings and nations and all creatures. It means a failure to recognise time as an epoch of death's worldly reign, a misapprehension of the ubiquity of fallenness throughout the whole of creation, and in turn, a blindness to imminent and recurrent redemptive signs in the everyday life of this world.[14]

What one finds in this use of scripture is something altogether less precise in its exegesis. The text becomes a catalyst for interpretation and a gateway to new understanding. What is demanded of the reader is imaginative participation in order to explore the ambiguities, tensions and problems that the text offers. For example, Stringfellow allows the imagery of the Apocalypse to be juxtaposed with the interpreter's own circumstances, whether personal or social, so as to allow the images to inform understanding of contemporary persons and events and to serve as a guide for action. In this process we find taking place the renewal of the mind which Paul describes in Romans 12.1–2.

In such imaginative and ethically oriented readings, the relationship to earlier scripture is oblique, as the biblical text is a springboard, or a creative frame of reference for the world which confronts the interpreter. It suggests a rather different approach to practical theological engagement, in which anecdote and analogy contribute to the pursuit of truth. Like the parables of Jesus, which have consistently refused to be tied down to one particular meaning, it offers a mode of moral reasoning that prompts and tantalizes in ways that are unpredictable in their effects and may offer those who persevere a means of understanding reality, and thereby illuminate the action and commitment on which they are already embarked.

Stringfellow offers such a distinctive modern voice in this respect that we conclude this chapter with an extended extract from his writing. It is the opening page of an article he wrote entitled 'The Representation of the Poor in American Society: A Subjective Estimate of the Prospects of Democracy'.[15] It presents a striking example of Stringfellow's contextual theology, and his insight into the inseparability of life, theology, and practice.

> After nearly ten years in which most of my practice as a lawyer has been among the indigent or those otherwise dispossessed or disowned by society, it has become impossible for me to think dispassionately or consider hypothetically or address academically the issues of the representation of the poor in politics and in the law in America. I suspect that there is, about these matters, no such thing as objectivity anyway; I know there is no option of neutrality about them. It would be pretentious for me to feign objectivity; it would amount to fraud to assert that I am neutral.
>
> Be cautioned, therefore, that in what follows I speak as a partisan – as someone with a definite viewpoint – though, in doing so, I trust, I thereby uphold the discipline of advocacy which is the venerable societal office of the lawyer.
>
> My viewpoint regarding the representation of the poor in society, especially in the realms of politics, legislation, administration of the law, and litigation, is, of course, informed by my own practice among the poor. No doubt every reader who is a lawyer is similarly positioned in relation to his own particular

experience in practice, whatever it happens to be, whether he is specifically conscious of that or not, unless he be some mere legal mechanic who forbears to reflect as a human being upon the work he does every day.

I am a Christian, moreover, which means that the focus of my attention in work, as well as everything else, is upon *this* world and the possibility and actuality in this world of mature human life in society. Biblically and empirically, the Christian concern is characteristically mundane, not spiritual. If there be preachers who none the less deny this world and vainly talk of other worlds or after lives, if there be ministers of institutional religion who spread a word that Christianity is bothered only with personalistic salvation and not with the corporate existence of mankind and there *are* legions of them – then they are either knaves or harlots: it is sometimes difficult to distinguish between the two. They had better read the Bible more avidly and the daily newspapers more discerningly, because both of these testaments bear witness that the scene of God's presence and vitality is this history in which men now live, with all its ambiguity, alienation, strife, controversy, and scandal.

7

Marriage and divorce

—◆—

In an MA seminar group we discussed the interpretation of
the texts in the New Testament about wives being submissive
to their husbands (Eph. 5.21–33, Col. 3.18–19, 1 Pet. 3.1–6).
The group was reluctant to accept that otherwise apparently
'normal' Christian men might deliberately use such texts to
justify their own violence against their wives – until one of the
members told us that her husband had done so for years . . .
[The woman explained] that her husband justified his beating
of her by claiming this was encouraged in the New Testament
texts.[1]

As the previous chapter showed, Blake was willing to criticize
specific elements within the Bible when they conflicted with its
wider message of a compassionate, loving God. In doing so he
was engaging in a form of Sachkritik, the approach to scripture
exemplified by Jesus, Paul, the early Church and (in principle at
least) Barth, the Pontifical Biblical Commission, Tom Wright
and the authors of the Windsor Report. Sachkritik is a willingness
to read the Bible in the light of the Spirit, and it is a faithful
form of interpretation: it has faith that God is bigger than a
book, and that engaging critically with that book will not mean
that the whole edifice of Christianity – God, Christ, Spirit, angels
and all – will come crashing to the ground. Christianity would
be a fragile religion indeed if brushing up against the real world
and human conscience left it in perpetual threat of implosion.

Feminist theology

Some of the biblical interpreters in this book – Winstanley, Denck, Stringfellow and the Liberation Theologians – interpret the Bible as a text that offers the possibility of human freedom and justice, and they do so in direct contrast to their contemporaries whom they see as using the Bible to justify exploitation and inequality. These writers are mainly concerned with exposing false readings and 'abuse' of the text by oppressors, while still regarding the Bible itself as 'benign'. However, other approaches to the Bible – such as those of feminist theology – are more suspicious that the oppressor is embedded within the text itself.

The Bible was written in a patriarchal culture, and has been interpreted predominantly in patriarchal cultures up to and including our own day. Those who are engaged in the struggle with the injustice of patriarchal social structures are therefore challenged by scriptures that embody and often endorse the very injustices that they are fighting against. Women's experiences and voices are not nearly as easy to find as men's in the Bible, and when they are found they may be as worrying as they are helpful. Moreover, the actual view of women which appears to have divine legitimation in the Bible is in itself problematic. The Bible has been used to legitimate the dominance of men in both the ecclesial and domestic spheres and also to legitimate a diminished estimation of the character, calling and abilities of women.

The actual text of the Bible carries both liberative and oppressive messages and claims. It is important to recognize that the same text that can be emancipating for one individual or group can be the justification for exploitation or the source of oppression for another. The Bible has been the source of emancipation and flourishing; but it has also been the cause of oppression and suffering. In short, when it comes to the question of the history and culture of injustice in 'Christian' societies the Bible itself is part of the problem. One particular feature of women's lived experience that must be faced in relation to the biblical text is the experience of violence. Violent treatment and sexual abuse of women is portrayed at many points in the Bible: the abuse of Lot's daughters, the murder of Jephthah's daughter, the rape of Tamar, the dismemberment of the unnamed woman in Judges 19, the violent sexual and anti-female imagery of Hosea 2, Ezekiel 16, and so on.

But it is not only a question of the way in which women are portrayed, or even the acceptance of patriarchally constructed relationships between men and women. It is also a question about the kind of God portrayed in the Bible. The images and language for God and the actions ascribed to God are predominantly male in character. The stereotypically masculine attitudes, capacities and actions depicted in the Bible (particularly the Old Testament) have historically been more highly valued and regarded as 'god-like' than their feminine counterparts. Moreover, in the history of the Church, God's authorized interpreters have so often been male, and the justification for this has been biblical, and also based on the very nature of God incarnated as a *man*: Jesus Christ.

All Liberation Theology privileges the voices of those who are not being heard, the voices of the oppressed. Rosemary Radford Ruether describes this as the 'prophetic principle', seen clearly in the prophets of the Hebrew Bible and the life of Jesus.[2] Through these prophetic individuals, religion that supports the oppressive status quo is challenged by God's message of justice and flourishing for the oppressed. Ruether sees this prophetic tradition as being in direct correlation with the critical principles of feminist theology, which recognizes and articulates the full humanity of women. Feminist biblical interpretation asks questions about what kind of identities women in Christian communities are forming as they engage with the Bible as it is mediated to them. It also discusses what forms of democratic and participative Bible interpretation will enable a helpful engagement between the text and the experience of women.

Marriage and divorce

Being a Christian does not mean defending every aspect of the Bible. As we have been suggesting throughout, the Bible is not a rule book, but a space within which we can explore our forms of understanding. The questions raised by feminist theology are a helpful way into thinking about how the Bible has also been a source of enormous suffering for countless people in the contexts of marriage and divorce. Marriage and divorce are high on the agenda of many Christians, not just because of the polarized nature of the debate about same-sex relationships. The issue of the propriety and sustenance of permanent relationships also remains a source of confusion and dissension. We address this issue with a different type of approach: rather than setting a case out, we provide an open-ended debate which functions, we hope, to draw attention both to the complex biblical attitudes towards marriage and divorce found in the Gospels, and to the complex set of life situations in the light of which we have to engage with these ideas. We have written this section as a dialogue not because we want to set up a straw man and then knock him down, but because we wish to articulate two different perspectives on the Bible. This dialogue is intended to be used as the basis for reflection, facilitated by using the questions following the case study.

Case study

A churchgoing woman had been in a marriage of thirty years. Though neither was having an affair, she and her husband gradually grew apart, and eventually the woman instigated a divorce. After the divorce, the woman entered a disastrous relationship, then spent several years on her own. The initial sense of liberation that she experienced following the divorce had quickly passed over, and she now felt unable to go to church due to the strongest feelings that she was no longer accepted there. These feelings were not unfounded: following the divorce she had been disowned by a number of friends and was left feeling enormous guilt. In time she started attending another church and eventually found someone she became very close to there. After a friendship of several years, they married.

Her adult children, who were evangelicals, greeted the new relationship – as they had the divorce – with outright rejection. In their view, there were clear Gospel passages (such as Matthew 5.29–32 and Mark 10.1–12) showing that their mother had committed, and continued to commit, adultery. They were deeply concerned for her spiritual welfare because they believed that she would be under condemnation for this ongoing adultery, and that no repentance for this sin was possible while she remained in the relationship. They felt therefore that it was their responsibility – out of love for their mother and concern for her spiritual welfare – to warn her that she was going to hell. They did not mean this in a metaphorical sense, but adopted the language used by Jesus himself in Matthew 5. The children's solution was that their mother should leave this new marriage forthwith and become celibate for the rest of her life. All but one of the children were united in their feeling on this matter; in accepting the mother's new relationship, this sibling was also rejected by the others. The rejection had been made for 'the sake of the gospel'.

In what follows we present a dialogue exploring two responses to this situation. They correlate roughly to 'conservative' and 'liberal' perspectives. We are not presenting them as 'right' and 'wrong' responses, but wish to suggest instead that both sides have insights, and that it is only through ongoing open discussion that we can begin to grasp the issues involved, and to recognize the human cost of our judgements.

Dialogue

It's not a complicated situation – the woman is in the wrong because she left the marriage too easily in the first case. She had a commitment to her husband and to God, and she threw these away because, basically, she got bored. People today enter marriage with no sense of commitment, and as soon as marriage gets tough they jump ship, thinking that the grass is greener on the other side of the fence. But they then get into another relationship – as happened to this woman – and go through the same thing all over again. They're simply not adequately committed to the vows they've made. That's not to say that some people aren't in relationships that they should have got out of a long time ago, like where there's abuse or ongoing infidelity, but in most cases it's a lack of sense of the sanctity of the vows made before God that lets them divorce. The overall Christian ethic on marriage is that you marry for life, and you don't enter marriage thinking 'I can get out of this if I don't like it.'

But the kids are cruel to her; surely the New Testament doesn't endorse that sort of rupturing of relationships?

It does seem hard, but the Bible is hard, and Jesus' teachings are explicit on this as the children recognize. In Mark 10 Jesus actually says 'Anyone who divorces his wife and marries another woman commits adultery against her. And if she divorces her husband and marries another man, she commits adultery.' This is exactly what has happened here. The wife instead of the husband is the instigator, but she has divorced and she is committing adultery by marrying the new husband. The children want the new relationship to be broken up so that the mother may be restored to Jesus, and that too is justified because as Jesus says in Luke 12.53, if families need to be broken up in order to follow him, so be it – sons against fathers, daughters against mothers.

You're oversimplifying the situation – you need to look at it in the context in which those passages arose. That discussion about divorce in Mark 10 which Jesus has with his learned opponents has been used to make marriage a sort of bedrock of the universe as God intended it, and has been treated as if it's the only thing in the Bible that speaks to the topic. I agree that taken out of context the words can seem to have only one meaning – that divorce is outlawed – but you need to see that strange debate for what it actually is: a learned debate between teachers about the grounds for divorce, not an endorsement of the institution of marriage.

So what? I don't see how that affects the meaning.

It affects it because Jesus is taking issue with the Law of Moses, whom he presents not as a channel of the oracles of God but as a human legislator, which is why Jesus says 'for your hardness of heart did Moses say this'. Mark 10 has all the features of rabbinic debate of the period in which a specific issue becomes the basis for legal disputation. That sort of theoretical discussion, as with all rabbinic debates, is not an absolute pronouncement on the matter, but part and parcel of the to and fro of application which is typical of all casuistry.

But Jesus' position is also confirmed by Paul in Corinthians.

Yes, Paul has reason to allude to this tradition and while it is true that his position reflects that element in the Jesus tradition there is none of the 'life-long commitment and indissolubility' in a verse like 1 Corinthians 7.15. Rather what we have here is Paul the rabbi dealing with the issue in typical rabbinic manner, negotiating the particularities of the situation in which the nascent Christian community at Corinth found itself.

You're diluting the meaning with context. The Gospels show a clear and direct affirmation by Jesus of marriage as a Christian institution, and they show God's endorsement of that form of relationship – and the family structure which comes through it – to be both the basis of society and part of God's kingdom.

*That's not the case. When Jesus talks about marriage and fam-
ilies in his teaching, his position is at best equivocal. As you have
said, he problematizes family ties by setting daughters against
mothers, and that attitude has deep roots in the early Church despite
being at odds with a growing acceptance of the family structure
in the second generation of the Pauline churches. When Jesus is
asked about the relationship of marriage and the coming kingdom of God, his answer indicates that marriage is something that
will disappear in the age to come 'when the inhabitants of the kingdom will be like angels'. He doesn't suggest that there will be no
sexual relations at that time, only that there will be no marriage.
So it's not surprising that in the early centuries of the Church, as
people attempted to live heaven on earth, some of them rejected
marriage because they saw it as being part of an order that had
passed away and not characteristic of the life of the kingdom of
God.*

So the future of the kingdom is one in which there is no commitment, just people having sex with whoever makes them feel
better? And presumably that's just tough luck for children who
need the stability that heterosexual marriage offers?

*The only commitment in the Jesus tradition is to the kingdom
of God, not to the institutions of this age. One might want to
emphasize the importance of commitment in the Jesus tradition,
but this should be about dealing with issues like the resolution of
conflict rather than upholding vows or institutions. Vows can and
should be renewable and renegotiable by consent, and they need
to be supported by a legal and social framework as they are in
the UK today, but that's all. The assumption that Jesus endorsed
marriage, that marriage is about monogamy, and that monogamous marriage is the Christian basis of social structures and
values just doesn't hold water.*

So what you're saying now is not just that divorce is OK, but
that the vows that explicitly state that they are for life, don't
really mean that they are for life?

I'm just saying that it's ironic that this supposed cornerstone of Christianity should contradict what Jesus said about the life of discipleship in the Sermon on the Mount. The marriage service is full of vows, and that flies in the face of the spirit of Jesus' injunction in Matthew 5.30–37 where he prohibits the swearing of oaths.

So presumably you think that not only does Jesus not endorse marriage, but that there's nothing to differentiate a marriage blessed by God from a civil ceremony?

There is a difference, but we need to think carefully about what that is. The difference centres on the priest's declaration 'that which God has joined together let no one divide'. This is an extraordinary claim that a human choice is none other than that which God desires, which is basically to claim that one knows the will of God. But how can we presume to know the will of God in respect to the deepest desires and longings of a couple, and how can some people claim to be able to distinguish that situation from, say, the case of two women who meet together to make vows one to another?

I don't understand why you have a problem with identifying human actions with God's actions. Aren't we discerning the will of God if we feel that being faithful to each other and to God is expressed through marriage? Besides, making this claim for marriage is entirely continuous with the Bible. Just to take one famous example, Jesus attended the marriage feast at Cana, and everything that's said in the Bible is in favour of marriage. Marriage, moreover, is the central metaphor used to describe the relationship between God and his people, and sexual infidelity is used as an appropriate way to describe infidelity to God.

That's right, sexual infidelity is famously used at the beginning of the book of Hosea to describe Israel's unfaithfulness to God. But it's not clear why sexual fidelity – rather than any other type of fidelity – should be the determining characteristic of marriage.

I'm not saying that marriage is about sex, or that you can't have a good marriage without sex, but it seems right that there is an idea of faithfulness within any kind of relationship, and not having sex behind your spouse's back hardly seems much of a demand in the context of the most special relationship that anyone has.

What the marriage service demands of an individual hardly does justice to the experience of life, as we all form bonds of mutual affection, support and the like which may well be more crucial sources of affirmation and life for us than our marriage relationships. Within our society that seems to be allowed, and those sorts of intimate intercourse are somehow all right, provided that they don't involve sexual intercourse. Why there should be something special about genital contact as the sole determination of the boundaries of appropriate intercourse is not so clear. There's an argument from natural law that can be made about sex leading to children, and there are economic reasons for sexual monogamy in cultures where women are in some ways the property of men to be transferred by an appropriate rite from one man (the father) to another (the husband). In the nomadic culture of the patriarchs such moments of transfer were important, but, to put it mildly, that was a different world.

But there are all kinds of reasons for sexual monogamy apart from just unwanted pregnancy, such as sexually transmitted diseases, and deep human feelings about the privacy of body parts and intimacy. What's more, the vows are made to each other, not just to God, so it's about commitment even in a civil relationship. A physical relationship is a giving of yourself, and giving someone else your body is the ultimate commitment. You say that the issue of sexual fidelity is a cultural one, but that doesn't help, because even if it were cultural, what you're asking is still impossible, as we can't simply step out of the cultures that have created us. Besides which, you could equally say that love is cultural, or the need to be with another person is cultural, which then negates your argument for the priority of intimacy whatever the social cost. But that's not the point here, as this isn't just cultural – sexual fidelity is endorsed repeatedly in the many biblical pronouncements against adultery in Exodus, Psalms and the New Testament, and the wedding service itself is looked over and endorsed by God.

OK – I do think that there is a strong sense that the Christian understanding of marriage is continuous with the drift of the Bible on that topic, and it's also true that the depiction of exclusivity in relationships between God and humans then gets projected on to marriage. What we have to ask ourselves, however, is whether the preoccupation with sexual intercourse as the criterion of infidelity is actually one that enables us to understand how best to embody the way of Jesus Christ in our context. The problem with Christian marriage is that there is a very particular understanding of commitment which means that the love, friendship and service that can characterize it, often over decades, suddenly count for nothing if adultery has taken place. It's true that adultery means offending against one of the Ten Commandments, but does this necessitate disintegration of a whole relationship – as it currently seems to in both civil and religious law?

The problem with the modern world is its constant criticism of the wisdom of the past and its inherited traditions. What makes our generation so superior in intellect and insight that we can turn our back on this institution which has served society so well? The disparaging of marriage is another example of modern hubris. Apart from the way in which it guarantees the fabric of society, marriage is actually a way of protecting women against exploitation by men, for it ensures that the ruthless do not get away with their self-centredness. To paraphrase the Book of Common Prayer, it is a remedy against misplaced desire and self-indulgence at the expense of the more vulnerable.

Questions

The questions that follow offer a way of approaching these issues without (as far as possible) presupposing that we have any clear answers. While we have a particular viewpoint, expressed quite clearly in other parts of this book, we have tried to avoid putting the questions in such a way that we load the dice towards particular outcomes. Of course, in setting up this kind of exercise there is an explicit presumption that we may challenge received wisdom, and that the Bible and its role is open to question and revision. That's a basic claim of this book.

- Even if we conclude that Jesus' view of marriage has been more or less accurately preserved by the Christian churches, does that have to be binding on us? After all, few of us follow Jesus' example with regard to the practice of exorcism, or for that matter his teaching on war, violence, vows and wealth.
- Is it possible to compile a coherent view of marriage from the Bible?
- If you can and have done so, can you stand back and offer a rationale for your selection and ordering of the priority of the biblical material?
- Are the differing attitudes to marriage in the different parts of the Bible suggestive of the fact that they reflect ancient cultural assumptions or preferences, and should ancient cultures that are very different from our own determine the way we approach the issue of long-lasting intimate relationships today?
- If one espouses a view which asserts that vows are renegotiable, how might that affect the upbringing of children?
- Christians have often considered that heterosexual marriage is built into the fabric of creation and that we as humans are monogamous by nature. We know that ancient philosophers like Aristotle used this kind of argument to explain that some

people were natural slaves and some natural masters. Is this argument from nature justifiable on the basis of the Bible?

- May we extrapolate from what Jesus said about divorce the supposition that he taught also the centrality of hetero-sexual, life-long monogamy?
- In explaining how we work out an understanding of and approach to intimate personal relationships, what is the relative weight we give to the Bible as compared with experience, and why do we consider this balance appropriate?

Reflection

The issues raised in this chapter affect the majority of people in Britain, whether Christians or not. Assumptions about the nature of life-long commitment and its viability are hardly ever questioned. Nonetheless, those who are most centrally involved with these issues do sometimes speak out on the subject. For example, Terry Prendergast, chief executive of Marriage Care, the Roman Catholic marriage preparation and counselling service, has recently written:

> Marriage means committing yourself to another and being faithful. The reasons why the sexual element of the relationship has remained so key are difficult to determine, while the notion of marriage – that one person will satisfy the other socially, physically, emotionally, psychologically and sexually over a very long period of time – is possibly problematic itself. Many believe that such a remit is impossible.[3]

Agonizingly, and often acrimoniously, Christians have had to face up to whether received wisdom towards issues like slavery, wealth and poverty, gender and race, to name but a few, can any longer be supported. It's common, when discussing such changes in attitudes, to quote the words of C. F. Alexander, creator of some of the British church's favourite hymns, whose 'All Things Bright and Beautiful' includes the following rationalization of social injustice:

> The rich man in his castle,
> The poor man at his gate,
> God made them, high or lowly,
> And order'd their estate.

We just assume today that Alexander was wrong about this, but her views were widely held in her day. We wouldn't want to support this any longer just because it can be proved from the Bible or because it coincides with what the Church teaches. In the case of marriage and other issues of sexuality it may be that the received wisdom is appropriate for our age (and indeed every age). What we need to do, however, is to understand why we think as we do, and not call each other names because we choose to ask ourselves questions about how and why we should accept that received wisdom and whether it is what God wants of us.

As we completed this book, the newspapers carried the story of the disqualification of a gay man from a leadership role in the Church of England because, in the judgement of a bishop, his lifestyle was not compatible with that expected of a Christian leader. The Bishop went out of his way to point out that this was not discrimination against gay and lesbian people and that the same moral criterion would apply if a heterosexual person was engaging in a sexual relationship outside heterosexual marriage.

When it comes to lifestyle, therefore, the Church appears to be able to live with egocentricity, selfishness, autocracy, even excessive wealth and membership of the House of Lords ('You know that among the gentiles those whom they recognize as their rulers lord it over them, and their great ones are tyrants over them. But it is not so among you'; Mark 10.42–43). All these things seem to be permitted, despite the warnings in the Bible about them. Yet when it comes to the breaching of the ecclesially authorized way of being sexually active (that is, with a member of the opposite sex, within the confines of marriage only), anything which transgresses this immediately disqualifies a person from leadership, even if that person is a gifted reconciler, pastor, preacher, teacher or administrator. Apparently these qualities count less than whether or not the individual in question displays the appropriate sexual conduct.

The Church of England is a national church and as such is willing to make compromises and be part of the corridors of power in order to bring the gospel of Christ to bear on decisions which affect ordinary people. Yet for too long it has been a glass house filled with individuals throwing stones at those who deviate from its elevation of heterosexual monogamy. It has thereby brought itself into disrepute by the contradiction between its preaching and its practice. This criticism is not made from a perspective of moral superiority: as academics we write from a comparably compromised institutional world that has an equally problematic relationship to 'life'. Rather, it is written to suggest that the Church – which clearly recognizes the need for compromise – should make its compromises across the board, accepting the task of doing what is 'good enough' and dropping its commitment to the sexual utopia which is embodied in the marriage service.

Instead of telling people what to do, Christians of all types might look to the example of Jesus who not only fraternized with 'sinners', but told his opponents that 'the tax-collectors and the prostitutes are going into the kingdom of God ahead of you' (Matthew 21.31). The failings of ecclesiastical institutions down the centuries better qualify them for solidarity with 'sinners' than for the censoriousness which is currently proclaimed by many of their leaders.

8

Concluding reflections

———◆———

There is a remarkable painting by Diego Velázquez in the National Gallery, London, entitled *Christ in the House of Martha and Mary*. It is reproduced on the front of this book.[1] It depicts a servant girl preparing a meal, accompanied by an older woman. The servant girl, looking somewhat surly and put upon, is very much in the foreground, but we do not know her identity. Nor do we know the identity of the older woman: is she a fellow servant in the household, or does she have a symbolic function, perhaps as an older incarnation of the serving girl, or as a representation of the serving girl's internalized sense of duty (along the lines of Freud's 'superego')? The old woman, in a didactic way, seems to be pointing – but to what? Is it to the scene in the right-hand corner of the picture, or to the lot of the young woman having to toil to make the meal for the unseen grandees who are taking it easy in another part of the house? What is that scene anyway? Is it a picture? Is it a mirror, reflecting events that are actually taking place somewhere behind the viewer? Or are we as spectators being asked to look as if through a window to a room beyond? The image appears to depict Jesus and Mary and Martha in the midst of the scene described in Luke 10. In that passage Martha remonstrates with Jesus for not caring about the fact that she is left to do all the toil while Mary sits at his feet learning, like a disciple, from the teacher. This, presumably, is the moment when, after remonstrating with Jesus, Martha receives her enigmatic word of reproach, which problematizes the life of drudgery against which she protests and which a latter-day Martha appears to be protesting against in the foreground. The eyes of Jesus are not unequivocally on Martha, however, and Mary hardly looks overjoyed at his words.

The scene in the foreground is mundane, while that in the background appears to open into that other world of the biblical text. The meaning of neither the contemporary scene nor the biblical scene is clear. What is clear is that there is a dialogical hermeneutic set up here – an interplay between the two scenes – and it is in our engagement with this interplay that meaning is to be found. In this respect the meaning of the picture is less important than the process of engagement it sets up. Through this challenging picture, Velázquez offers us a paradigm of the way in which we might engage with the Bible: his painting neither rejects the Bible nor gives it unquestioned prominence as if it were prescriptive and determinative of what is going on in the contemporary world (here indicated by the foreground scene). Indeed, Velázquez has problematized the idea of the Bible as something that simply explains or dictates how life should be. Instead, the picture beckons us to attend to the young woman and the circumstances that place her in this position of drudgery, and in doing so it implicitly questions our neat acceptance of Jesus' own word in the Lucan story as the last word on the topic.

The foregrounding of life with the Bible as a backdrop reminds us that discipleship in the Spirit is altogether more tentative, more dangerous and less predictable than most institutional Christianity has been comfortable with. The ways of discipleship will not be identical in different times and places: Philippi in the middle of the first century CE will be different from New York or São Paulo in 2008. Of course, a modicum of predictability and the habitual is necessary for our common life, but that is no excuse for the backward-looking lifestyle that characterizes most of both ancient and modern Christianity. Hermeneutically the New Testament suggests that we should be ready to explore and experiment and run the risk of making mistakes, provided we continue to maintain ways of relating, however confident we are that we are right.

A reiterated theme in our book has been that the exercise of imagination (or whatever reading strategies we choose to pursue) is not separate from the practice of discipleship. Liberation Theology has put solidarity with (and sustenance of) the vulnerable and oppressed – whoever they are – back at the centre of the life of the church. 'I desire mercy not sacrifice,' says the prophet, words echoed by Jesus himself (Matthew 9.9). In the Gospel the critical meeting with Christ, surprising as it may seem to all concerned, turns out to have been an encounter with the needy and impoverished (Matthew 25.31–45). Ministering to the Son of Man and engaging in the costly process of dealing with conflict are fundamental to any understanding of practical discipleship, and, indeed, of any theology. They require of us appropriate ways of engaging with the Bible to match the new situations of commitment and action with which we are now being confronted. That involves mutual edification and criticism, which ultimately depends on owning and accepting difference and diversity in the community which is journeying together. We may find this in seeking to live with each other, accepting our differences. This will always involve processes of growth and not just the application of clear-cut rules.

Our emphasis on context and the questioning of absolute perspectives is a point of view at the heart of one of the most influential writers of Christianity, Augustine. But Augustine inherited from Tyconius his view of the Church as a body of people whose eternal destiny was known only to God, and the acceptance that the righteous would be separated from the unrighteous only at the last judgement. Judgement was reserved for God alone, and it was incumbent upon all Christians to find ways of relating to each other in love as they journeyed towards the truth, the fullness of which would be revealed only at the End of Time. The way in which we journey together is more important than the guarding of a truth that we have only partially grasped. It is not up to us to separate the wheat from the tares (Matthew 13.29); that should be left to God. In the meantime we must learn to practise charity, that gift which persists into the age to come because it is above all else the quality we dare to assert most especially about God and ourselves (1 Corinthians 13).

The stories of Jesus depict a wandering preacher who didn't discriminate who his table companions should be and didn't set rules and regulations about who should be part of his circle. Tax-collectors, prostitutes and people who were thought of as notorious sinners by his society were included. Unsurprisingly, accusations circulated that he was the friend of gluttons, drunkards and sinners, and even that he was inspired by Beelzebub. He commended forgiveness of sins and taught his disciples to forgive sins in parallel with God. Wherever that sort of action and mutual engagement with difference and perceived wrong takes place, so Matthew's Jesus is reported to have said, there his presence is to be found (Matthew 18.20): if the Church wants to follow Jesus, it will take to heart the practice and forms of relating that he commends.

Glossary

Exegesis and eisegesis

These two related words describe ways of engaging with a text, or indeed with the interpretation of anything. Exegesis is about 'getting out of a text only what it contains'. In other words, this is the task which allows the text to be understood without any agenda of the interpreter affecting the quest for the text's meaning. It is the interference of the interpreter's agenda which can lead to 'eisegesis', where the interpreter uses a text as a peg on which to hang their own agenda. Throughout this book we question whether there can be a neat distinction between the two. Attempts to explain the literal meaning of the text don't really get us very far and even the most sophisticated interpreters are bringing something else to a particular text (whether it's another text or one's own agenda) to make sense of it.

Eschatology

Eschatology is literally the discussion of the end of things: of history, of the future of the world, of the destiny of the individual. In traditional Christian thought eschatology is about heaven, hell, death and judgement, even though in the New Testament hope had a more social and worldly dimension. We have used 'eschatology' to describe the biblical hope for a time of peace and justice on earth, which is what Christians pray for when they pray for the coming of God's kingdom.

Hermeneutics

'Hermeneutics' is used in two ways. First, it describes what we do when we think about the ways in which we interpret, and when we try to explain to ourselves and others how we have gone about making sense of the Bible. It describes the process whereby we stand back and reflect on our reading and why we relate to biblical texts in the ways in which we do. Second, it refers to the ways in which study of the ancient texts which make up the Bible might be related to our modern world and the various means, whether philosophical or sociological, by which we explain how ancient ideas and practices may apply in the modern world.

Sachkritik

Sachkritik is a form of interpretation in which meaning is disclosed as the reader struggles to get at what a text is really about, without assuming the literal meaning is the final or total meaning. Retrieving an original meaning is not the point. Instead, the reader seeks understanding in the relationship between his or her own situation – biographical, political, social – and the text itself. The text illuminates the world of the reader, the world of the reader illuminates the meaning of the text. For example, many first-century texts unquestioningly accept slavery. This might stand out as a problematic issue to a twenty-first century reader in a way that wouldn't have been visible to the actual writers of those texts (who took this to be part of the natural order of things). Sachkritik is a contextually driven reading, so that the reader tries to understand a writer's words as well, if not better, than the original writer. So, it does not bracket out the experience of the interpreter, but equally does not allow that to so condition the engagement with the text that there cannot be mutual dialogue between the two. This process is open to any one who wishes seriously to engage with the text. It does not depend on experts to tell less educated readers what they should know about the author's intention or the historical context; neither, for that matter, does it depend on the ability to abstract principles which can then, and only then, be applied by modern readers.

Notes

1 The Bible for gluttons, drunkards and other 'sinners'

1 Quoted in John F. Kippley, *Sex and the Marriage Covenant: A Basis for Morality* (Ft. Collins: Ignatius Press, 2005), pp. 359–60.
2 Estimated UN figures for 2006 <http://data.unaids.org/pub/GlobalReport/2006/2006_GR_CH02_en.pdf> accessed 15 April 2007.
3 The Laing Lecture 1989, and the Griffith Thomas Lecture 1989. Originally published in *Vox Evangelica*, 1991, 21: 7–32 <http://www.ntwrightpage.com/Wright_Bible_Authoritative.htm>
4 N. T. Wright, *Scripture and the Authority of God* (London: SPCK, 2005), pp. 91–2.
5 Wright's hierarchical understanding of interpretation (with the bishops at the top) can be seen, for example, in the concluding pages of *Scripture and the Authority of God* (pp. 101–2).
6 Albert Schweitzer, *The Quest of the Historical Jesus* (London: A & C Black, 1931), p. 401.

2 'Christian' responses to same-sex relationships

1 *The Windsor Report 2004: The Lambeth Commission on Communion* (London: Continuum, 2004), sections 54–6.

3 Interpretation in context

1 This point was made with great force by the Anabaptists in the sixteenth century and more recently in John Howard Yoder's *The Politics of Jesus* (Grand Rapids: Eerdmans, 1972), a work that has had a greater effect on contemporary Christianity than most books written in the last fifty years.
2 Augustine, *On Christian Teaching*, trans. R. P. H. Green (Oxford: Oxford University Press, 1997), p. 68.
3 See, for example, J. Ashton, *Studying John* (Oxford: Clarendon Press, 1994), pp. 206–7, and K. Stendahl, 'Contemporary Biblical Theology', in *The Interpreter's Dictionary of the Bible*, ed. G. A. Buttrick et al. (Nashville: Abingdon, 1962), vol. 1, pp. 418–32.

4 N. Lash, *Theology on the Way to Emmaus* (London: SCM Press, 1986) and also Stephen C. Barton, 'New Testament Interpretation as Performance', in *Life Together: Family, Sexuality and Community in the New Testament and Today* (Edinburgh: T & T Clark, 2001), pp. 223–50.

5 J. L. Houlden (ed.), *The Interpretation of the Bible in the Church* (London: SCM Press, 1995).

6 Karl Barth, *The Epistle to the Romans*, trans. E. C. Hoskyns (Oxford: Oxford University Press, 1933), pp. 2–10.

7 See the entry in the Glossary. Also see the discussion of Sachkritik in Robert Morgan's introduction to the new edition of Rudolf Bultmann's *Theology of the New Testament* (Waco: Baylor University Press, 2007).

8 Houlden (ed.), *Interpretation of the Bible in the Church*, p. 50.

9 Houlden (ed.), *Interpretation of the Bible in the Church*, p. 50.

10 Houlden (ed.), *Interpretation of the Bible in the Church*, p. 51.

11 Houlden (ed.), *Interpretation of the Bible in the Church*, p. 81.

12 J. Ashton, *Studying John* (Oxford: Clarendon Press, 1994), pp. 206–7, our emphasis. The contrast between understanding and application is paralleled (though coming from a very different philosophical starting point) in Nick Wolterstorff's distinction between 'authorial discourse interpretation' and 'performance interpretation' in his 1993 Wilde Lectures: *Divine Discourse: Philosophical Reflections on the Claim that God Speaks* (Cambridge: Cambridge University Press, 1995).

13 Raymond Brown, *The Community of the Beloved Disciple* (New York: Paulist Press, 1979).

14 See James Barr, 'The Literal, the Allegorical, and Modern Biblical Scholarship', *JSOT*, 1989, 44; and B. Childs, 'James Barr on the Literal and the Allegorical', *JSOT*, 1990, 46.

15 A modern-day version of Augustine's position can be found in Abba Matta El-Meskeen (founder of the Monastery of St Macarius, Wadi El-Natrun, Egypt) printed in their monthly journal *St Mark*, November 1981.

4 Liberation Theology

1 Carlos Mesters, 'The Use of the Bible in Christian Communities of the Common People', in N. K. Gottwald and R. A. Horsley, *The Bible and Liberation*, revised edition (London: SPCK, 1993), pp. 14–15.

2 Quoted in C. Rowland and M. Corner, *Liberating Exegesis* (London: SPCK, 1990), pp. 13–14.

3 Examples of material produced by the Archdiocese of São Paulo may be found in Rowland and Corner, *Liberating Exegesis*, pp. 7ff.

4 Unpublished translation of material accompanying *Parábolas de Hoje a Ovelha Perdida* (São Paulo: Edições Paulinas, no date).

5 Gustavo Gutiérrez, *The Power of the Poor in History* (London: SCM Press, 1983), p. 57.

6 C. Boff, *Theology and Praxis* (Maryknoll: Orbis Books, 1987), p. 149.

5 Christian radicals: Denck and Winstanley

1 See A. Bradstock and C. Rowland, *Radical Christian Writings: A Reader* (Oxford: Blackwell, 2002).

2 See Gerald West, *The Academy of the Poor* (Sheffield: Sheffield Academic Press, 1999).

3 *Recantation*, 1, in Clarence Bauman, *The Spiritual Legacy of Hans Denck: Interpretation and Translation of Key Texts* (Leiden: Brill, 1991), p. 251.

4 Bauman, *Spiritual Legacy of Hans Denck*, p. 26.

5 'Whether God is the cause of evil', in Bauman, *Spiritual Legacy of Hans Denck*, p. 113.

6 *Concerning True Love*, 78, in Bauman, *Spiritual Legacy of Hans Denck*, p. 187.

7 This is a powerful example of Sachkritik, building on the similar hermeneutical moves in Matthew 22.38–40 and Romans 13.10.

8 For details of Denck's life see Bauman, *Spiritual Legacy of Hans Denck*.

9 Information on Winstanley's life is taken from J. C. Davis and J. D. Alsop, 'Winstanley, Gerrard (*bap.* 1609, *d.* 1676)', *Oxford Dictionary of National Biography* (Oxford University Press, 2004) <http://www.oxforddnb.com/view/article/29755> accessed 15 April 2007.

10 See the chapter on Winstanley in Bradstock and Rowland, *Radical Christian Writings*, pp. 120–37.

11 G. Winstanley, *The New Law of Righteousness* (January 1649), quoted in Bradstock and Rowland, *Radical Christian Writings*, p. 123.

12 Winstanley, *The New Law of Righteousness*, quoted in Bradstock and Rowland, *Radical Christian Writings*, p. 123.

13 Quoted in Bradstock and Rowland, *Radical Christian Writings*, p. 124.

14 Quoted in Bradstock and Rowland, *Radical Christian Writings*, p. 124.

15 Davis and Alsop, 'Winstanley'.

16 From G. Sabine, *The Works of Gerrard Winstanley* (New York: Russell, 1965), p. 162.

17 From Sabine, *The Works of Gerrard Winstanley*, p. 153.

6 Christian radicals: Blake and Stringfellow

1 All Blake quotations are from *The Complete Poetry and Prose of William Blake*, new revised edition, ed. David Erdman (New York: Bantam Doubleday Dell Publishing Group, 1997).

2 T. S. Eliot, *The Sacred Wood: Essays on Poetry and Criticism* (London: Methuen, 1950), p. 155.

3 *The Complete Poetry and Prose of William Blake*, p. 614.

4 *The Complete Poetry and Prose of William Blake*, p. 618.

5 *The Complete Poetry and Prose of William Blake*, p. 844.

6 *The Complete Poetry and Prose of William Blake*, p. 211.

7 From the *St. Louis Post-Dispatch*, 20 November 1969, reproduced in *Reporting Vietnam: American Journalism 1959–1975* (New York: Library of America, 2000), pp. 418–19.

8 W. Stringfellow, *An Ethic for Christians and Other Aliens in a Strange Land* (Waco: Word, 1973), p. 72.

9 W. Stringfellow, *My People is the Enemy: An Autobiographical Polemic* (New York: Holt, Rinehart & Winston, 1964).

10 Stringfellow, *An Ethic for Christians*, p. 13.

11 Stringfellow, *An Ethic for Christians*, p. 152.

12 Stringfellow, *An Ethic for Christians*, p. 24.

13 Stringfellow, *An Ethic for Christians*, p. 21.

14 Stringfellow, *An Ethic for Christians*, p. 55.

15 W. Stringfellow, 'The Representation of the Poor in American Society: A Subjective Estimate of the Prospects of Democracy', *Law and Contemporary Problems*, 1966, 31:1, Antipoverty Programs (Winter), pp. 142–51.

7 Marriage and divorce

1 Zoë Bennett, *Introducing Feminist Perspectives on Pastoral Theology* (Sheffield: Sheffield Academic Press, 2002), pp. 34, 64. See also Zoë

Bennett and Christopher Rowland in Paul H. Ballard and Stephen R. Holmes (eds), *The Bible in Pastoral Practice: Readings in the Place and Function of Scripture in the Church* (London: Darton, Longman & Todd, 2005).

2 Rosemary Radford Ruether, *Sexism and God-Talk: Toward a Feminist Theology* (Boston: Beacon, 1983), pp. 22–4; 'Feminist Interpretation: A Method of Co-Relation' in Letty Russell (ed.), *Feminist Interpretation of the Bible* (Philadelphia: Westminster, 1985), pp. 111–24.

3 Terry Prendergast, *The Tablet*, 28 April 2007, p. 11.

8 Concluding reflections

1 Its theological significance is discussed by J. Boyd and P. Esler, *Visuality and Biblical Text: Interpreting Velázquez' 'Christ with Martha and Mary' as a Test Case* (Florence: Olschki, 2004).

Suggestions for further reading

Readers of this book will understand if our suggested reading is less about the content of the Bible and more about how we read it.

Both of us continue to learn from William Blake's poetry and art about how we read the Bible. Blake has been the unseen partner throughout this book. We would like to think that he may be a similar companion to others, and to this end each of us has written a book seeking to make his hermeneutics more accessible: Jonathan Roberts's *William Blake's Poetry* (London: Continuum, 2007) is an introduction to his work, while a fuller discussion of his hermeneutical methods can be found in Christopher Rowland's *Blake and the Bible* (London: Yale University Press, 2008). *William Blake: The Complete Illuminated Books* (ed. David Bindman, London: Thames and Hudson, 2000) provides beautiful colour facsimiles of his illuminated works in all their variety.

The radical tradition that Blake inherits is described in Christopher Hill's *The World Turned Upside Down* (Harmondsworth: Penguin, 1972), which provides an extraordinary account of dissent in England during the English Revolution, and which shows people reading texts in ways remarkably similar to those of the first Christians.

Looking back to earlier forms of biblical interpretation, the imaginative engagement with the Bible which is such a part of the liberationist and Ignatian method has its antecedents in the kind of imaginative exegesis practised by monks in the Middle Ages. This has been illuminated in a number of books by Mary Carruthers, particularly *The Book of Memory* (Cambridge: Cambridge University Press, 1990). Ignatian spirituality itself offers a means to engaging with life and the Bible, and there is no better introduction to its practice than Gerard W. Hughes's *God of Surprises* (London: Darton, Longman & Todd, 1985).

It is not so clear where the radical tradition goes after Blake; however, we would recommend a number of books by later writers. Albert Schweitzer's *The Quest of the Historical Jesus* (London: A & C Black, 1931) is a classic piece of modern New Testament scholarship remarkable both for its insight into what was going on in nineteenth-century biblical scholarship, and for its scintillating reconstruction of the Jesus of history. We may not agree with all of the details but few would dissent from the basic outline of what Schweitzer wrote, particularly with regard to the effects of eschatology on the history of early Christianity and the shape of Christianity.

No one has written such a book for the twenty-first century, though the late John O'Neill began the task in *The Bible's Authority* (Edinburgh: T & T Clark, 1991), a book which urgently needs to be reprinted. Of course, what is distinctive about Schweitzer's work is that Schweitzer the scholar merges with Schweitzer the disciple of Jesus. Just before the First World War he left behind a brilliant career both as a musician and as a biblical exegete to work as a missionary doctor in West Africa.

In a similar vein, William Stringfellow's commentary on the book of Revelation, *An Ethic for Christians and Other Aliens in a Strange Land* (Waco: Word, 1973), was written from within the context of the Vietnam War. It's an extraordinary work, though perhaps more accessible is the anthology of his work, *A Keeper of the Word: Selected Writings of William Stringfellow* (ed. Bill Wylie Kellermann, Grand Rapids: Eerdmans, 1996).

For a more general discussion of different hermeneutical strategies, Paula Gooder's new book *Searching for Meaning: A Practical Guide to New Testament Interpretation* (London: SPCK, 2007) introduces different ways of engaging with the Bible as an enormously diverse set of texts. A discussion of the 'plain sense' of scripture can be found in John Barton, *The Nature of Biblical Criticism* (Louisville: Westminster John Knox Press, 2007), pp. 69–116.

A 'must' for any community interested in conflict resolution and reconciliation is Carolyn Schrock-Shenk (ed.), *Mediation and Facilitation Training Manual: Foundations and Skills for Constructive Conflict Transformation* (Akron: Mennonite Conciliation Service, 2000). This contains a wealth of material relating to the practicalities of the work of conflict resolution based on years of experience in personal, social and international peace-making.

Further information about other ideas in the book may be found in Christopher Rowland, *The Cambridge Companion to Liberation Theology*, 2nd edn (Cambridge: Cambridge University Press, 1999), and Andrew Bradstock and Christopher Rowland, *Radical Christian Writings: A Reader* (Oxford: Blackwell, 2002).

Index

All Bible chapter and verse numbers are shown in italic type.

Abraham 18
Acts 70
Acts *2* 62
Acts *2.17* 8
Acts *11.17* 19
Acts *15.20* 20
adultery 92, 93
Alexander, C. F. 100–1
Anabaptism 62ff.
apocalypse 73, 84f.
Aquinas 4
Ashton, John 40, 42
Augustine 33, 42, 105
authority 16

Babylon and Jerusalem 84f.
Barth, Karl 22, 23, 24, 25, 36ff.,
    66, 88
Bauman, Clarence 65
Beelzebub 17, 106
Benedict XVI *see* Ratzinger,
    Joseph Alois
Blake, William 73ff., 88, 114
body of Christ, the 80
Boff, Clodovis 59, 60
Brazil 46ff.
Brown, Raymond 42
Bultmann, Rudolf 38

Calvin 37
Cana 96
Carruthers, Mary 114

CEBs (Communidades Eclesiais
    de Base) 47
Christ: character of 8; imitation
    of 22
Christianity: conservatism of
    30–1, 61
Colossians *3.18–19* 88
communicative interpretation 44
communism 70
contextual theology ix, 43, 46;
    modern suspicion of 40f.
contraception 4
Corinthians *see* First Corinthians;
    Second Corinthians
Cornelius 19

Daniel 68
Denck, Hans 63ff., 72, 89
Diggers, the 71
discernment 26, 27ff.
discipleship 20, 44
dispensationalism 32

eisegesis, definition of 107
Eliot, T. S. 22, 76
Enlightenment, the 42
Ephesians *5.21–33* 88
Ephesians *6.12* 82
Erasmus 63
eschatology, definition of 107
exegesis ix, 39; as actualization
    36; ancient and modern

forms of 35f.; and application 35f.; critical self-awareness in 43; definition of 107; and imagination 41f.; literal 31ff.; modern 34f.; modern academic 42; patristic and medieval 33; Reformation 34
Exodus *21.23–25* 79
Ezekiel *16* 90

Fall, the 69f.
First Corinthians *2.10–16* 26, 64
First Corinthians *7.15* 94
First Corinthians *8* 20
First Corinthians *11* 18
First Corinthians *11.1* 22
First Corinthians *12* 8, 18
First Corinthians *13* 106
First Corinthians *13.10* 29
First Corinthians *13.12* 27
First Corinthians *14* 27
First Corinthians *14.34* 30
First John *4.7–21* 66
First Peter 30
First Peter *3.1–6* 88
forgiveness of sins 78, 79
Freud, Sigmund 103
Friere, Paulo 50, 51

Galatians 17
Genesis 69
Genesis *15.6* 18
Genesis *17.11–14* 18
Genesis *21.4* 18
Genesis *23—24* 18
Gooder, Paula 115
Gutiérrez, Gustavo 54

Harlem 82ff.
hermeneutics ix, 8; definition of 107

Hill, Christopher 114
historical reconstruction 41
HIV/AIDS 4
homosexuality *see* same-sex relationships
Hosea *2* 90, 96
House of Lords 101
Hughes, Gerard W. 114

imagination 10, 38–9, 41–2, 79ff.

James *2* 66
Jeremiah *22.16* 55
Job *1.6* 78
John *3* 55
John *7.14–24* 59
John *11.49* 56
John *16.12* 7
John *16.13* 7
John, Gospel of 16, 42
John, Jeffrey 13, 14, 75
John, letters of *see* First John
John Paul II, Pope 4
Judges *19* 90

King, Martin Luther 82f.

Lambeth Commission 42
Lash, Nicholas 36, 41, 55
last judgement 7, 45, 105
Liberation Theology 10, 38, 45ff., 84, 89, 105
'little ones' 57f.
logos 15
Luke *7.33–34* x, 5, 12
Luke *10* 103
Luke *11.14ff.* 17
Luke *12.53* 93
Luke *12.56* x, 3
Luke *15.1–2* x, 58

Luke *15.1–7* 58
Luther 63, 65

Manz, Felix 67
Mark *1.22* 16
Mark *1.44* 12
Mark *2.6* 17
Mark *2.16* 12
Mark *2.23ff.* 12
Mark *3.22ff.* 17
Mark *8.31* 56
Mark *8.38* 56
Mark *9.31* 56
Mark *10* 93, 94
Mark *10.1–12* 92
Mark *10.33–34* 56
Mark *10.42–43* 101
Mark *10.45* 56
Mark, Gospel of 31
marriage and divorce 88ff.
Martha and Mary 103f.
Matthew *5.21ff.* 17
Matthew *5.29–32* 92
Matthew *5.30–37* 96
Matthew *6.33* 62
Matthew *7.21f.* 58
Matthew *9.9* 105
Matthew *10.42* 58
Matthew *11.18–19* x, 12
Matthew *11.25* 8, 56, 57
Matthew *12.50* 59
Matthew *13* 59
Matthew *13.1–23* 32
Matthew *13.29* 106
Matthew *18* 54
Matthew *18.1–4* 57
Matthew *18.12–14* 50
Matthew *18.20* 106
Matthew *18.21–22* 79
Matthew *22.36–49* 38, 111
Matthew *25* 7

Matthew *25.31–45* 45, 57, 105
Matthew *25.40* 59
meaning, literal 33
Mesters, Carlos 47
monogamy 97, 102
Moses 16, 17, 38, 66, 94
My Lai *see* Vietnam

Nicodemus 55

O'Neill, John 115

parables of Jesus 86
parable of the lost sheep 50ff.,
    57ff.
parable of the sower 32
parable of the wheat and the
    tares 59
parable of the woman and the
    lost coins 58
Pastoral Epistles 30
Paul 17, 18, 20
Peter 17, 19, 20, 62, 79
Peter, letters of *see* First Peter
Philippians *2.6–11* 22
Philippians *3.9* 21
Pirke Aboth 17
Pitt, James 48
Pontifical Biblical Commission
    36, 39f., 88
Prendergast, Terry 100
psychotherapy 43

radicals, Christian 61ff.
Ratzinger, Joseph Alois 48
realized eschatology 71
Reformation, the 13, 34, 63
Revelation *2.7* 7, 68
Roberts, Jonathan 114
Robinson, Gene 13, 14, 75
Romans *8* 26

Romans *8.3* 66
Romans *12.1–2* 86
Romans *13.9–10* 38, 111
Romans *14.1–4* 29
Romans, Barth's commentary on 36f.
Rowland, Christopher 114, 115
Ruether, Rosemary Radford 90

sabbath observance 12
Sachkritik ix, 28, 31, 38ff., 88; definition of 108
same-sex relationships 13ff., 27, 28, 38, 91
Samson 80
Satan 78
Schrock-Shenk, Carolyn 115
Schweitzer, Albert 9, 114, 115
Second Corinthians 21
Second Corinthians *3.6* 25
Sermon on the Mount, the 17, 96

Shakespeare 6
Sobrino, Jon 40
Spirit, the 3, 25ff., 63ff.
Stendhal, Krister 36
Stringfellow, William 76, 81ff., 89, 115

table fellowship 17–18
Theologia Germanica 65
Tyconius 105
Tyndale 63, 64

Velázquez 103ff.
Vietnam 81f.
violence against women 88f.

Windsor Report, the 23, 24, 25, 39, 48, 88
Winstanley, Gerrard 67ff., 76, 89
Word of God, the 77
Wright, Tom 6, 14, 24, 25, 39, 42, 88